FLYBOYS

OVER

HAMPTON ROADS

FLYBOYS
OVER
HAMPTON
ROADS

GLENN CURTISS'S
SOUTHERN EXPERIMENT

Amy Waters Yarsinske

Charleston London

THE
History
PRESS

Published by The History Press
Charleston, SC 29403
www.historypress.net

First published 2010

Manufactured in the United States

ISBN 978.1.59629.972.6

Library of Congress Cataloging-in-Publication Data

Yarsinske, Amy Waters, 1963-
Flyboys over Hampton Roads : Glenn Curtiss's southern experiment / Amy Waters
Yarsinske.
p. cm.
ISBN 978-1-59629-972-6
1. Atlantic Coast Aeronautical Station (Newport News, Va.)--History. 2. Curtiss, Glenn
Hammond, 1878-1930. 3. Newport News (Va.)--History, Military--20th century. 4.
Hampton Roads (Va. : Region)--History, Military--20th century. 5. Aeronautics, Military--
History--20th century. I. Title.

UG634.5.A78Y37 2010
358.4009755'5209041--dc22
2010035936

CONTENTS

INTRODUCTION

G lenn Hammond Curtiss's establishment of the Atlantic Coast Aeronautical Station at Newport News, Virginia, at the end of 1915, what many then called the aviation giant's southern experiment, was driven by climate and war. But it soon became as much about the people who came and went and the aircraft that came off the land and lifted from the water and into the history books. Curtiss's flying school and experimental station was all but gone by 1922, eclipsed by the new naval air station across Hampton Roads at Sewell's Point and the army's Langley Field in Hampton, both of which station manager Captain Thomas Scott Baldwin predicted would collocate with Curtiss's Newport News location as soon as it opened. This seldom-mentioned Curtiss station was marked by great achievement and incredible tragedy.

Curtiss's tenure in Hampton Roads was punctuated by legendary aviators, remarkable aircraft and record-breaking flights. In less than six years, Curtiss's record of achievement at the Atlantic Coast Aeronautical Station quickly reached national and international significance. But there was more. While Hampton Roads certainly played a pivotal role in aviator training and as host field to record-setting flights before and during World War I, it played an even greater role in the development of new aircraft. More than a flying school, Curtiss established here an experimental test facility through which any number of one-of-a-kind aircraft were assembled, tested and evaluated. The Atlantic Coast Aeronautical Station, developed on a landlocked twenty-acre tract just east of Newport News's municipal small boat harbor in the fall of 1915, had all the right stuff.

Aviation giant Glenn Hammond Curtiss, photographed about 1911, first visited Norfolk, Virginia, in 1910 with his old friend and internationally famous aeronaut Captain Thomas Scott Baldwin. The two were scouting a location for Curtiss to build an aircraft test facility. When Norfolk said no, they looked at a site in Newport News, across Hampton Roads, that might provide the service conditions to test seaplanes. Though it took several more years for Curtiss's test facility and flight school to come to fruition on a twenty-acre site at Newport News's municipal small boat harbor, what unfolded over a period of seven years became the stuff of which legends are made. No one human being did more to further aviation than Curtiss. His reach was worldwide. *Courtesy of the George Grantham Bain Collection, Library of Congress Prints and Photographs Division.*

Curtiss first wanted to locate a flying school in Norfolk, what he'd determined just then to be Hampton Roads' central city. During a visit to the city in 1910, accompanied by Captain Baldwin, Curtiss identified several outstanding sites, but Norfolk wasn't amenable to development of an aeronautical station. Though disappointed, Curtiss continued to look regionally. Since Curtiss was then in the process of designing a larger flying boat, he was looking for a suitable site that proffered warmer water year round to test it under actual service conditions. After Norfolk turned him down, he and Baldwin took the ferry across Hampton Roads. He found what he was looking for at the tip of Newport News Point. While the site was ideal, the timing wasn't. Curtiss and Baldwin returned to Hammondsport empty-handed.

Though Curtiss wasn't unhappy with his Buffalo, New York manufacturing and flight school operation, it also wasn't a perfect marriage. Buffalo was close to shipping lanes and, at least until the weather turned bitterly cold and the water froze over, a prime location on Lake Erie to test flying boats. The decision to expand to Buffalo had also been driven by the city's abundance of skilled labor and the fact that it was close enough to Hammondsport, New York, Curtiss's home and original company headquarters, to quickly receive material used to build his aircraft. Curtiss came to depend on the city's capable tradesmen, reliable materials and easy access to Lake Erie. What he'd failed to consider was something Buffalo couldn't give him: year-round testing on the water.

Despite Buffalo's shortcomings, there wasn't much of a rush to open a flying school and experimental station south of the Mason-Dixon line in 1910. American aviation could hardly be called an industry prior to World War I. Curtiss Aeroplane Company was the only enterprise turning out aircraft in any quantity, and those were small, and in 1914 his Hammondsport plant employed only six men. The Burgess Company in Marblehead, Massachusetts, was building limited lines of hydroaeroplanes, and the American Wright Company, headed by Orville Wright until his retirement in 1914, had been tinkering so long with new designs that its production had virtually come to a standstill. Other than the Glenn L. Martin Company in Los Angeles, there were no other aircraft manufacturers in the United States, and much of what they produced was experimental.

There were few, if any, privately owned aircraft. The average person couldn't afford one. Most didn't have money to take flying lessons, either. But none of this kept Curtiss flying schools from becoming an important part of budding United States Army and Navy aviation programs, predating the official start of both services' flight school curricula. Years before the United States declared war in the spring of 1917, the navy and army contracted with Curtiss, the Wright brothers and Burgess to teach handpicked officers from each service to fly. The navy continued to send officers to Curtiss and the others even after it established the naval aviation camp at Greenbury Point, Maryland, in 1911. The sea service's new aviators used Curtiss and the other companies to advance their flying skills and to learn more about how aircraft worked. Curtiss's teaching regime was tailored to everything a new navy pilot might need to know on the ground and in the air.

By 1912, Curtiss's Model F flying boat, slightly modified to military specifications and called the Curtiss MF flying boat, was being used as a short-range naval reconnaissance aircraft, and Curtiss was about to introduce its first experimental JN Jenny military tractor plane, an aircraft destined to become wildly popular with army aviators. By 1915, Glenn Curtiss had manufacturing plants and flying schools at Hammondsport and Buffalo in New York and in San Diego, California. When he opened a flying school in Toronto that year, it was Canada's only properly accredited program until it closed at the end of 1916 and thus the only one to produce certified graduates at the end of pilot training. The school maintained a lengthy waiting list of prospective pilots, most of them already accepted as aviation candidates by the British Royal Flying Corps, precursor to the Royal Air Force, while others had tentative acceptance to the Royal Naval Air Service, subject to each of them obtaining a private pilot license. Faced with weeks of waiting for a slot to open up at Toronto, eligible Canadian men signed up for flight instruction in the United States, and they weren't all headed to Curtiss's flight schools at Hammondsport, Buffalo and San Diego. They were signing up for lessons at the American Wright Company at Dayton, Ohio, and taking lessons from prodigious aviator Eddie Stinson and those like him. There were many eager young men who wanted to join British and French flying squadrons overseas.

The war in Europe quickly surmounted Curtiss's existing manufacturing and test sites, and he ran out of room at all his flying schools. The six employees he had in 1914 became two hundred in 1917. Curtiss's impetus to get Newport News up and running was driven by prequel. England was Curtiss's biggest customer after the war broke out in 1914. The British needed aircraft and the men to fly them. Curtiss promptly hired away top engineer Benjamin Douglas Thomas from England's Sopwith Aviation Company. Thomas designed and produced Curtiss's first JN model, an enjoining of the Curtiss J model, his first tractor plane, with the N model, Curtiss's standard aircraft. The JN, popularly called the Jenny, had a tandem cockpit and was used as the training plane of choice by the American and British armies. But he got his biggest boost in sales to England from aircraft designer and collaborator Royal Naval Air Service Wing Commander John Cyril Porte, who saw the development of Curtiss's largest flying boats as an opportunity for the British navy to increase its capability in the air.

Before the war, Curtiss and Porte had worked together at Hammondsport on the design of a large twin-engine flying boat for Rodman Wanamaker, the Curtiss H-1 *America*. The *America* was the first aircraft capable of nonstop transatlantic flight, but it never got the chance. The war in Europe put an end to transatlantic attempts until 1919. Despite the lost opportunity with *America*, the two continued to collaborate. Recalled to military service, Wing Commander Porte, in a move for which he was

Captain Thomas Scott Baldwin created a motorized balloon in 1900 using a Glenn Curtiss motorcycle engine. This aerodynamic cigar-shaped hydrogen-filled bag became the dirigible *California Arrow*, shown here, which took its first controlled circular flight in the United States on August 3, 1904, when aeronautical engineer and aviator Augustus Roy Knabenshue took it aloft at the Louisiana Purchase Exposition in Saint Louis. *Courtesy of the Library of Congress Prints and Photographs Division.*

later criticized, encouraged his superiors to purchase Curtiss H-4 flying boats, a military version of their earlier twin-engine, 100-horsepower *America* flying boat that Porte promptly modified. He refitted the H-4 with a new hydrodynamic hull that made taxiing, takeoff and landing far more practical. He renamed it the Felixstowe F.1. He also swapped out underperforming 160-horsepower Curtiss engines for high-performance, 250-horsepower Rolls-Royce Falcons. Porte then modified the hull of the larger Curtiss H-12 Large America flying boat, creating the Felixstowe

"Captain Tom" Baldwin was photographed at the controls of an aircraft he built after a Curtiss pattern that he called the *Red Devil*. The picture was taken about 1910, five years before he came to Newport News, Virginia, to run Glenn Curtiss's flying school and aircraft experimentation facility. Baldwin flew the *Red Devil* in several aviation exhibitions, including an Asian tour that lasted nearly six months. *Courtesy of the George Grantham Bain Collection, Library of Congress Prints and Photographs Division.*

F.2, which was greatly superior to the original Curtiss aircraft. Under his supervision, the Felixstowe Seaplane Experimental Station continued to enlarge and improve the design of Felixstowe aircraft independent of Curtiss through the F.3 and F.5 variants. Porte's final design was the five-engine Felixstowe Fury triplane, also known as the Porte Super Baby.

With a stiff wartime requirement to train flyers parked on his doorstep and aircraft that couldn't wait weeks to be tested, Curtiss had a decision to make. Arguably, Hammondsport and Buffalo were problematic. During the winter months, both sites froze out training, and prospective pilots lingered for weeks without anything to do. Testing came to a halt. Curtiss needed a warmer place to train pilots and test aircraft, and he needed it right away. Curtiss again broke out his plan for a Newport News aeronautical station. There, he'd establish a rookery for airmen that had never before been seen in the mid-Atlantic. The city land Curtiss espied for the Atlantic Coast Aeronautical Station stretched from the apex of Jefferson Avenue at the ferry

Early bird aviator James Cairn "Bud" Mars was photographed during an aviation meet in Erie, Pennsylvania, organized by Captain Baldwin and held less than a month after their return from overseas. Mars flew on July 14, 1911, and contrary to popular reporting associated with this date, he was not fatally injured when his plane plummeted to the ground. Though seriously hurt, he recovered. Born March 8, 1876, and raised on the lakes of Michigan, the man billed as "Mars, the Lion-Nerved Daredevil" became Baldwin's student at the tender age of sixteen. Before he met Curtiss, Mars and Israel Ludlow had built several huge man-carrying kites at the 1907 Jamestown Exposition and took them aloft for experiments over Hampton Roads. By 1910, he'd made his way to Hammondsport, New York, where Curtiss taught him to fly his early pusher aircraft. During World War I, he was a first lieutenant in the United States Army Signal Corps Aviation Section. He died in Los Angeles on July 25, 1944. *Courtesy of the George Grantham Bain Collection, Library of Congress Prints and Photographs Division.*

docks for a little over a mile before looping north to Salter's Creek. He laid out a landplane field and dock facility congruent with the municipal small boat harbor. This time, he also had a champion to make the process go quickly.

Connecticut millionaire Irving Hall Chase, who claimed his initials stood for "I Have," heard about Curtiss's proposal for the land in Newport News and negotiated with city officials for the site. The Newport News Municipal Industrial Commission agreed to lease the land to Curtiss for one dollar a year. But there was, as always, something in it for Chase. The land deal included a cold storage facility for the handling of fish and oysters on land adjacent to Curtiss's aeronautical station. The negotiation

Three Japanese military representatives observed Curtiss airplane tests in 1912, within a year of Baldwin's return from his tour of Asia and the Pacific, and they would be present again in 1916 in Newport News to observe and train. The importance of Japan's interest in aviation for military application and the consequent rise of Japanese air power that followed cannot be overstated. From the left are Imperial Japanese Army Colonel Yoshitsugu Saito, a lieutenant general appointed in April 1944 as head of the Forty-third Division on Saipan; unidentified; Imperial Japanese Navy Captain Tokutaro Hiraga, in 1912 the naval attaché to the Imperial Japanese Embassy in Washington, D.C., and promoted to rear admiral before his death on May 13, 1919; and Imperial Japanese Army Colonel Kazutsugu Inouye, the Japanese military attaché in Washington who rose rapidly through the ranks to major general. Inouye was Japan's military attaché in Washington for most of the decade. Inouye led a similar delegation to Newport News on May 9, 1916. *Courtesy of the Library of Congress Prints and Photographs Division.*

was a coup for Chase and a victory for Curtiss. But Curtiss needed someone to run it.

Curtiss turned to Captain Tom Baldwin. He trusted him. He relied on him. Baldwin was the dean of America's early birds, with a reputation established long before Curtiss became interested in aviation. Born on June 30, 1860, in Quincy, Adams County, Illinois, a detail confirmed by his June 11, 1888 passport application, Baldwin was a good choice to run a combination flight school and experimental station. Baldwin sported an impressive resume. By the turn of the twentieth century, he

Curtiss's decision to locate an experimental facility and flying school south of the Mason-Dixon line was largely precipitated by climate and war. Curtiss received a big boost in aircraft sales to England with the help of a good friend, Royal Navy Air Service Wing Commander John Cyril Porte, shown here with Curtiss about 1915. Just before war broke out in Europe in 1914, Curtiss and Porte collaborated on the design for a large flying boat, which they planned to fly across the Atlantic. The aircraft was called *America*. Given his close association with Curtiss, Porte knew that soon Curtiss would develop larger and faster flying boats that would exponentially increase the British navy's capability in the air. But Curtiss needed warmer water to do it. *Courtesy of the George Grantham Bain Collection, Library of Congress Prints and Photographs Division.*

was so well known that his contemporaries considered him the country's leading aeronaut. Baldwin was the originator of the parachute and was the first man to dare descend in one, a feat he first accomplished in San Francisco on January 30, 1885. He earned the title "Father of the Modern Parachute." For many years after his first parachute descent, Baldwin flew and manufactured balloons, dirigibles and aircraft. Between July and September 1888, he toured England, where he was a sensation. In total, Baldwin made thirty-eight ascensions and parachute drops in larger British cities, eleven of them in London. Five years later, in 1893, Baldwin appeared at the Chicago World's Fair, where he set up a demonstration of the first balloons owned by the United States Army. Yet despite his fame and considerable achievement as a balloonist, Baldwin wasn't fulfilled.

Baldwin had earlier begun building a motor-powered dirigible in California but was experiencing great difficulty procuring an engine to propel it forward. The engine had to be both compact and imponderable, yet powerful enough to drive a huge cigar-shaped gasbag through the air. To his knowledge, no one manufactured an engine that

The Atlantic Coast Aeronautical Station was choked with curious onlookers almost every weekend. Anxious crowds watched Curtiss instructors, most of them also experienced test pilots, take off and land. The star attraction on the weekend Frank Conway took this picture was the Curtiss L-type triplane, visible just to the left of the large hangar building. While the L-type never saw action in World War I, it was prototyped for the United States Navy and had been aloft during limited test flights just before the war's end. Spectators from Norfolk and Portsmouth boarded the ferry in Norfolk and came ashore at the municipal small boat harbor. Visitors from farther away bought passage on steamers from Washington and Baltimore and other points north and south. *Courtesy of the author.*

fit his specifications. By chance encounter, he met the man who would revolutionize his thinking.

Certainly by 1903, Glenn Curtiss had become the nation's foremost motorcycle constructor and racer, and his Hammondsport hometown was thus the hub of that industry. While Curtiss made it big in the motorcycle business, Baldwin built a reputation as a builder of balloons and as a temerarious aeronaut and international personality. But the two men hadn't met yet and possibly wouldn't have met at all had Baldwin skipped a trip to Los Angeles. During a meet in the city, Baldwin heard the sound of an engine that got his attention. A young man rode up on a motorcycle powered by a two-cylinder engine. The Curtiss motorcycle was exceptional, but it was the engine that Baldwin wanted to see. After close inspection, Baldwin read the name on the motor: G.H. Curtiss Manufacturing Company. He placed an order for one, but after several months passed and he still hadn't received it, Baldwin traveled to Hammondsport to find out why he'd heard nothing from its owner. Curtiss explained that it would take money he didn't have to build the engine Baldwin needed for his airship. Baldwin promptly funded the project, and Curtiss's workers immediately commenced building a two-cylinder, five-horsepower dirigible engine.

Baldwin's aerodynamic cigar-shaped hydrogen-filled balloon became the dirigible *California Arrow*, which took its first controlled circular flight in the United States on August 3, 1904, at the Louisiana Purchase Exposition in Saint Louis. Baldwin didn't fly it. His 225-pound frame made him too heavy to safely board and operate the dirigible, so he hired aeronautical engineer and aviator Augustus Roy Knabenshue to take his place. Twenty-nine-year-old Knabenshue was a slight-built 130 pounds. After this flight, Baldwin earned the title "Father of the American Dirigible." But more important than any sobriquet or fancy title, he'd gained an important collaborator: Glenn Curtiss.

With this milestone behind them, Curtiss constructed several engines for Baldwin in the years that followed the *California Arrow*'s successful flight, Curtiss himself going aloft with Baldwin on several occasions. Though the two had become fast friends, Curtiss didn't demonstrate much interest in aviation matters beyond building a motor here and there for Baldwin. Curtiss's interest continued to be motorcycle design and manufacture. It is a matter of public record that on January 24, 1907, Glenn Curtiss rode one of his motorcycles over a measured mile at a speed of 136.3 miles per hour at Ormand Beach, Florida, a feat that led the *Chicago Daily News* to call him the "Fastest Man on Earth."

Curtiss's passion for wings wasn't ignited until the 1906 Aero Club Show in New York, and it would be a slow burn. The Glenn H. Curtiss Manufacturing Company put out a display of its lightweight engine at the show, one similar to a motor he'd built for another Baldwin dirigible, *City of Portland*. The engine drew considerable curiosity from a white-bearded man, who asked Curtiss many questions about it. He wanted to know if it was possible to build and install such an engine on a kite-like contraption capable of taking off the ground carrying a man. Curtiss's reply was a curt "maybe." But he put the idea out of his head. Dr. Alexander Graham Bell, the man who'd asked the question, didn't. The man who invented the telephone was clearly captivated by the possibility of flight and wanted to know more. Yet he could also tell that Curtiss wasn't interested, not just then. Bell invited Curtiss to his laboratory near Baddeck, Nova Scotia, to witness a series of

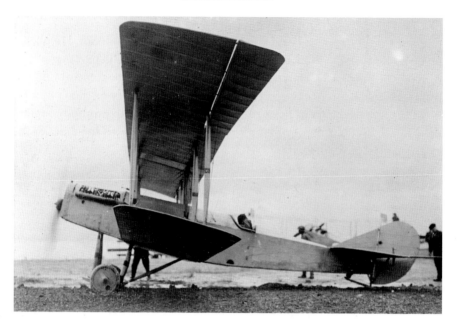

This is a single-seat Curtiss R-type biplane photographed by Frank J. Conway at the Atlantic Coast Aeronautical Station in early 1916. His initials appeared on the photograph, lower right, as "F.J.C." He also used "Conway" and "F.J. Conway" to identify his work. Conway was employed as a Curtiss Aeroplane and Motor Company photographer. *Courtesy of the Library of Congress Prints and Photographs Division.*

Frank Conway took what may be the first aerial photographs of Hampton Roads from a Curtiss F-boat flown by Walter Lees on December 29, 1915. The photographs in this sequence begin with several overhead and oblique pictures of the Atlantic Coast Aeronautical Station, discernible in the foreground. *Courtesy of the author.*

This picture of Newport News Shipbuilding and Dry Dock Company was also taken on December 29, 1915. A battleship of the United States Navy is at the dock, joined by an assortment of civilian and military ships under construction and others in the yard for repair. *Courtesy of the author.*

flight experiments that might change his mind. After the visit, Curtiss was sold. Shortly after, Curtiss devoted most of his time to aircraft research and development.

Though Bell closed the deal at Baddeck, Baldwin opened the door by getting Curtiss to build a dirigible motor. Whether Curtiss realized that he'd just sold his first engine for aviation use when he built Baldwin's *California Arrow* motor isn't as important as what came later. The relationship that sparked between Curtiss and Baldwin worked, and the friendship endured. After Baldwin's workshop was destroyed in the 1906 California earthquake, he moved his operation to Hammondsport, where he'd have unfettered use of Curtiss's plant for experimentation and construction of airships and, soon enough, aircraft. There on the edge of Lake Keuka rose "The Aerodrome," Baldwin's headquarters, laboratory and factory. He had much work to do.

Baldwin's *California Arrow* demonstration sent ripples through the army. Brigadier General James Allen, chief of the United States Army Signal Corps, stood below and watched Knabenshue fly it. Allen was so impressed by what he'd seen that he approached Baldwin to develop the dirigible for

Stewart Wellesley "Andrew" Cogswell, one of Curtiss's first and primary instructors and test pilots at Newport News, gave United States Army Major (later Brigadier General) William "Billy" Mitchell his first flying lesson on September 4, 1916. Born in Halifax, Nova Scotia, on January 2, 1891, the son of Arthur Wellesley Cogswell and Helen Maude Lithgow, he learned to fly at Curtiss's Hammondsport, New York facility in 1912 and was employed by the Curtiss Aeroplane Company as a flight instructor and test pilot, moving from one Curtiss facility to another until the United States entered World War I. During the war, he was chief flight instructor for the United States Army Signal Corps Aviation Section, which later became the United States Army Air Corps. When Frank Conway took Cogswell's picture in the fall of 1916, the station had already had several aircraft mishaps, one of them nearly fatal to Cogswell. Most of these early pilots' lives were short-lived. They'd die in fiery crashes. They'd die pinned under a heap of wreckage. But not Cogswell. He died on August 21, 1956, in Daytona Beach, Florida, and while he had not lived a particularly long life by today's standard, he'd also escaped the fate that befell many pilots of his era: he didn't die in his airplane. *Courtesy of the author.*

army use. The signal corps offered to pay $10,000 for a practical means of dirigible aerial navigation and awarded Baldwin the contract. He delivered a ninety-five-foot airship, powered by a Curtiss engine of novel design, in 1908, and it was accepted and designated SC-1, the signal corps' first dirigible. The SC-1 established the template for all dirigibles of its era. Lieutenants Frank Lahm, Thomas Selfridge and Benjamin Foulois were taught to fly it. By the time Baldwin finished his work on army dirigibles, Curtiss had become a famous aviator in his own right. Baldwin, perhaps by force of habit, put Curtiss's work and career ahead of his own. He'd followed Curtiss's rise

The Curtiss JN-4D Jenny, shown here at Newport News in 1916, was the product of collaboration. This aircraft combined the best features of two aircraft, the Model J and the Model N, both designed by British aircraft engineer Benjamin Douglas Thomas under contract to Curtiss. Both models were two-seat tractor aircraft powered by a Curtiss OX engine, which was also new at that time. The Model J, the first predecessor to the Jenny, debuted on May 10, 1914, and the Model N followed shortly after. Curtiss built fewer than two hundred Model J and Model N trainers for the United States Army and Navy before he decided, in 1915, to produce the JN series. *Courtesy of the Sargeant Memorial Room, Norfolk Public Library.*

to fame closely, accompanying Curtiss to exhibitions and meets across the country, often making arrangements and providing prompts and advice. But he didn't give up on his own projects at The Aerodrome.

In the spring of 1910, Baldwin built the first plane with steel framework and called it the *Red Devil*. It used a twenty-five-horsepower, four-cylinder Curtiss engine that was later replaced by a Curtiss V-8 motor. Baldwin flew it at an air meet in Kansas City, Missouri, on October 7, 1910, and the next day he flew it at Belmont, New York. Baldwin convinced Curtiss to put together a world tour in December 1910 featuring the *Red Devil* that included exhibition pilots James Cairn "Bud" Mars and Tod Shriver. The tour traveled through the Pacific and Asia, stopping in the territory of Hawaii, the Philippines, Japan and China, where large numbers of people saw an airplane for the first time. The *Red Devil* was, in truth, the first aircraft to fly in many of the locales it was flown.

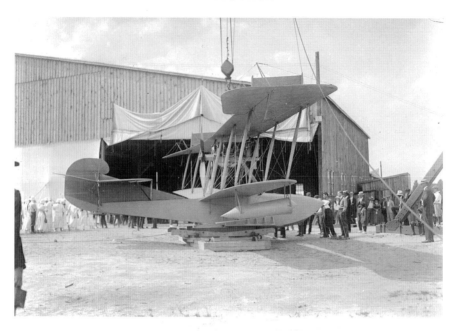

An unfinished Curtiss flying boat, called an F-boat, was brought out of its hangar for the Atlantic Coast Aeronautical Station's weekend crowd to see. The aircraft is not the model F-boat, later designed for the United States Navy, which had an overhanging top wing and inter-wing ailerons. This aircraft has neither. The photograph was taken in 1916, nearly two years before Curtiss made modifications to this original pusher flying boat, which he first introduced in 1912. The Curtiss F-boat is considered the first successful flying boat. *Courtesy of the Sargeant Memorial Room, Norfolk Public Library.*

Baldwin's overseas tour sparked tremendous interest in aviation. But nowhere was interest more piqued than Japan. Baron Yoshitoshi Tokugawa, a twenty-seven-year-old first lieutenant in the Imperial Japanese Army Engineer Corps, set a Japanese record with the Blériot on April 23, 1911, flying forty-eight miles in one hour, nine minutes and thirty seconds. Tokugawa's achievement came on the heels of Baldwin's tour of Japan. The following year, 1912, Japanese naval aviation was begun with the purchase of three Curtiss A-1 Triad seaplanes, which used both retractable wheels and floats and became the world's first successful amphibian. The A-1 Triad first flew on January 26, 1911, at San Diego, California, and shortly thereafter became the United States Navy's first airplane when the sea service bought it on July 1 of that year. Curtiss had much success selling this aircraft and its variants and successors to the British, Russian, German and, of course, Japanese navies within a year of its introduction.

After returning from his tour of the Pacific and Asia, Baldwin began testing a new aircraft at Mineola, New York, similar to a basic Curtiss pusher but

Victor Carlstrom, Curtiss's chief flight instructor and test pilot, is pictured in the cockpit of a Curtiss JN-4D Jenny at Newport News, Virginia, in 1916. Frank Conway took the photograph. *Courtesy of the author.*

fashioned, like the *Red Devil*, from steel tubing instead of wood. The aircraft was built for Baldwin by brothers Charles Rudolph and Adolph Wittemann of Staten Island, New York, and was powered by a sixty-horsepower Hall-Scott V-8. It was capable of sixty miles per hour. Baldwin named this new aircraft the *Red Devil III*, and thereafter each of his designs was called a Baldwin Red Devil. Baldwin's creation made news on October 12, 1913, when Tony Jannus flew actress Julia Bruns in a Red Devil during a *New York Times* derby. Baldwin's aircraft work wasn't limited to development of his own aircraft. Collocated with Curtiss, Baldwin helped him develop one of the most important features of flying boats: the pontoon fitted under the wingtips.

During the summer of 1914, as fighting erupted in the sky over Europe, Baldwin went abroad to observe and study dirigibles and airplanes in warfare. Baldwin's experience made him an outspoken advocate of greater use of aircraft as an essential part of the military. When he got home, Baldwin returned to dirigible work and designed the navy's first successful model, the DN-1, contracted on June 1, 1915, but not delivered by the Connecticut Aircraft Company until December 1916. Though Baldwin was still tethered to the navy's dirigible project, Curtiss asked him if he'd manage his Newport News flying school and flight test facility. He said yes.

The Curtiss JN-4D Jenny two-seat biplane was one of the most popular aircraft of all time. Although the JN-4 series was technologically unremarkable, it was significant in that it was the first mass-produced airplane and was manufactured in larger numbers than any other American aircraft up to that time. The Jenny proved itself a dependable military trainer. After the United States entered World War I, it was used to train about 95 percent of all prospective American and Canadian pilots. *Courtesy of the Sargeant Memorial Room, Norfolk Public Library.*

The Atlantic Coast Aeronautical Station was Curtiss's Felixstowe. The work that would be done there stood to revolutionize the design of future Curtiss aircraft. As a flight school, it would turn out more airmen than any other location in the country. Captain Baldwin declared it ready for business on December 10, 1915, but the staccato of hammers would be heard for several weeks to come as construction workers finished the station's main hangar and outbuildings. When Baldwin opened the station to the public on December 29, curious spectators showed up in droves, their presence recorded by Curtiss Aeroplane Company photographer Frank J. Conway, the first of thousands of photographs he took of the Atlantic Coast Aeronautical Station.

Curtiss's Newport News flight test facility left the door open for Baldwin to collocate an aircraft factory nearby. He investigated the possibility but couldn't identify skilled workers to build aircraft. The southeastern United States didn't have the tradesmen to do the work, and the cost of relocating skilled aircraft workers was too high. A skilled aviation worker in Curtiss's

Bertrand Blanchard "Bert" Acosta was assigned very early to the Atlantic Coast Aeronautical Station as a flight instructor and test pilot. Acosta was one of the most gifted pilots any of his fellow airmen had ever known, but his penchant for women, alcohol and stunts earned him the sobriquet "Bad Boy of the Air." He won the 1921 Pulitzer Trophy Race, in which he set a new speed record of 197.8 miles per hour. He was Rear Admiral Richard Byrd's copilot on the remarkable June 29, 1927 transatlantic flight that took place barely two weeks after Charles Lindbergh's famous crossing. He became front-page news as an anti–Francisco Franco mercenary in 1936 during the Spanish Civil War when he, Frederic Ives Lord and Eddie August Schneider signed on to organize the Yankee Squadron. But he lived hard and died young. Born on January 1, 1895, in San Diego, California, Acosta died on September 1, 1954, of tuberculosis at the Jewish Consumptive's Relief Society sanatorium in Colorado. He is in many photographs taken by Conway at Newport News. *Courtesy of the George Grantham Bain Collection, Library of Congress Prints and Photographs Collection.*

There is no name to go with this aviator's photograph. Frank Conway took his picture within the first year of Curtiss's Newport News flying school's opening. He photographed every pilot, student pilot, military and naval officer, American and foreign government official, personality and aircraft that ever came through Curtiss's Newport News station. He took thousands of photographs, of which just a few hundred remain. The United States Army alone put over one thousand officers and enlisted men through flight training at Newport News. During World War I, this was a big number. *Courtesy of the author.*

Buffalo plant made between fifty to sixty dollars per week. This was not, to be clear, an aviation mechanic who maintained aircraft already in service, but the man who assembled it. Baldwin couldn't find a location or the labor to do the job, and Curtiss dropped any plan to put a factory in Hampton Roads.

Thus, Baldwin turned his attention to getting the flying school operational and his experimental facility ready to go to work testing Curtiss's latest aircraft. But for both he had to hire the best instructor and test pilots. No Hollywood casting director could have been so lucky. His first two hires were Victor Carlstrom and Walter Edwin Lees. Carlstrom was the country's foremost test pilot, and Lees turned out to be the best instructor pilot Baldwin ever had, a sentiment later shared by the United States Army. Carlstrom and Lees would soon teach stage star Vernon Castle and the flamboyant army aviator Harold Marcellus "Buck" Gallop. But they would not be the only legendary airmen to grace the station. There were Eddie Stinson, Billy Mitchell, Bert Acosta, Jimmy Johnson and so many others. The men who

Glenn Curtiss's Toronto flight school maintained a lengthy waiting list of prospective student pilots, most of them already accepted by Royal Flying Corps and Royal Naval Air Service as flight candidates on the condition that they obtain their private pilot certification. When they couldn't get into Curtiss's Canadian training program, prospective Canadian flyers looked to private flight schools in the United States, including Curtiss's Hammondsport, Buffalo and San Diego locations. Those filled up fast. With Newport News up and running, Canadians came in large groups, usually about thirty at a time. This is a class of Canadian pilot candidates, photographed by Frank Conway in the spring of 1916 at Newport News. *Courtesy of the author.*

came and went were a who's who of early civilian and military aviation, including major World War I army aces and squadron commanders and members of the L'Escadrille Americaine (quickly renamed the L'Escadrille Lafayette), not to mention hundreds of Canadian, British, French, Finnish, Russian, Estonian, Latvian, Lithuanian and Japanese aviation candidates who found their way to Newport News. The United States Navy also sent dozens of its first naval aviators through basic flight training there, including members of the Harvard Flying Unit. But the men didn't get all the glory. Two of America's top female pilots, Ruth Law and Neta Snook, left their mark there, too.

Soon nearly a century will have passed since Captain Thomas Baldwin declared Curtiss's Newport News aeronautical station open and ready for business. This narrative, fifteen years in the making, is a record of what time forgot. But like all great stories, this one is only as good as the sum of its parts. Aviation pioneer Glenn Curtiss's contribution to his industry has been recognized and repeatedly honored since his death on July 23, 1930. But this is not the case with his Atlantic Coast Aeronautical Station, an important yet little-known chapter in American aviation history that was eclipsed by war and later dismissed as a minor footnote.

What happened at Newport News was far from small potatoes. The story begins in the fall of 1915, on the cusp of America's entry into World War I, and ends with the first theft of an aircraft in the United States. In the middle of it all are daring young men (and women) and their flying machines, their record-setting flights, their fame and sometimes the heartbreak of loss that was unavoidable and expected. Curtiss's southern experiment did not have to be open long to make a big first impression.

1
MR. CURTISS COMES CALLING

There was only a hint of fall in the air on the morning of October 29, 1915, when Harold Marcellus "Buck" Gallop picked up his morning edition of the *Daily Press* newspaper and began to look it over. There were headlines from far-off Europe in large type. More stories about the war, he thought. But it was a war the United States probably wouldn't enter, not just then. President Woodrow Wilson had promised it, so it must be true. Gallop moved on to page two. What he saw made him grip the page tighter. The article read:

> *Captain Thomas Scott Baldwin, inventor and experimental aviator of New York City, will build and experiment with a hydroaeroplane at the municipal boat harbor, he having secured permission from the municipal industrial commission to erect temporary buildings and shops at the harbor site. If Captain Baldwin's experiments are successful, it is possible that an aviation factory will be established in or near the city, probably at the harbor. Indications are that the work will begin immediately. The aviator selected Newport News as the base of his operations, it is reported, because the climate here is more equitable than any other place on the Atlantic Coast and there is a good amount of sunshine during both the winter and summer.*

Gallop was just as eager to learn to fly an airplane as any of the young men wait listed at private flight schools in Canada and across the United States. Those men wanted to join the Royal Flying Corps and duel the Germans, whose exploits in the sky over Europe sold newspapers in the United States.

Glenn Hammond Curtiss, posed here with his company's JN-4D Jenny biplane about 1916, was a driving force behind the creation of the Aerial Experimental Association in 1907. Less than two years later, on March 20, 1909, he and Augustus Moore Herring cofounded the first American aircraft company, Herring-Curtiss Company, which was shortly thereafter renamed the Curtiss Aeroplane Company in 1910. When the latter went public on January 13, 1916, it was renamed the Curtiss Aeroplane and Motor Company, the marriage of the Curtiss Aeroplane Company of Hammondsport, New York, and Curtiss Motor Company of Bath, New York. Curtiss Aeroplane and Motor Company is how his business is referred to most often in this narrative. *Courtesy of the George Grantham Bain Collection, Library of Congress Prints and Photographs Division.*

German aces Rittmeister Manfred von Richthofen, Oberleutnant Ernst Udet and Hauptmann Oswald Boelcke were shooting up the competition. But so was Canadian ace William Avery "Billy" Bishop; he would end the war with seventy-two victories. Bishop's combat record made him England's top ace of all time. But Gallop didn't picture himself slugging it out in a dogfight with Richthofen. Maybe others did, but not him. He just wanted to be part of something bigger than himself, and Baldwin's reputation and the start of a flying school in Newport News got his heart pounding.

The people of Newport News weren't unfamiliar with aircraft. Eugene Ely made his famous flight from the deck of the armored cruiser USS *Birmingham* (CL-2) on November 14, 1910, in Hampton Roads. A year before Baldwin began work on the Atlantic Coast Aeronautical Station, the newspapers reported that hydroaeroplanes were being launched and recovered from the armored cruiser USS *North Carolina* (ACR-12) in Hampton Roads and the Chesapeake Bay. One of the *North Carolina*'s aircraft had even fallen into the bay and was lost. Curtiss's decision to

Mr. Curtiss Comes Calling

Newport News's municipal small boat harbor developed quickly after the arrival of Glenn H. Curtiss's Atlantic Coast Aeronautical Station, which included the Curtiss Flying School and a flight experimentation facility. The placid, recreational inlet shown here soon became home to aircraft and new industries, which developed along the road to the aviation field. This and many of the other photographs contained herein were taken by Curtiss Aeroplane and Motor Company photographer Frank J. Conway between 1915 and 1922. *Courtesy of the author.*

collocate a flying school and experimental station in a region in which the United States Navy maintained a strong fleet presence and the army kept quarters at Fort Monroe put Baldwin's operation where it was most visible to the military. But it also made it vulnerable. Baldwin predicted that the army would locate a flying field in proximity to Curtiss's aeronautical station at the municipal small boat harbor. He said as much in the December 10, 1915 *Daily Press*, the same day he announced the station open for business: "It is practically certain that Captain Baldwin's judgment will be vindicated by the location near the city of a government Army Aviation Station, which will be the largest school of its kind in the world." Baldwin was prescient. But neither he nor the reporter had any way of knowing that an unscrupulous Elizabeth City County landowner would be a spoiler to the army's plan. Langley Field didn't develop just then because the landowner asked an outrageous price for her farmland. When it couldn't get the land right away, the army first developed a field in Florida, later renamed Homestead Air Force Base, located about thirty

Frank Conway took this picture looking through woods and wetlands toward the municipal small boat harbor and the makings of Curtiss's aeronautical station, then under development on the Newport News waterfront at Salter's Creek in 1915. *Courtesy of the author.*

miles from Miami. Langley didn't get its official start until the United States entered World War I.

In the fall of 1915, concern that his aeronautical station would one day be eclipsed by nearby navy and army facilities was the least of Captain Baldwin's concerns. He'd contracted Newport News carpenter Randolph Tucker Wood to build the main hangar and outbuildings on the Curtiss tract at the municipal small boat harbor. When Curtiss arrived on New Year's Day 1916 to spend several days inspecting the aeronautical station's testing plant, he reported later that he'd been satisfied with what he found. He found the school the same. That Curtiss found his Newport News station "first rate" and expected to pursue an expansive aircraft testing plant far south of his Hammondsport headquarters was significant. "The location is ideal for water flying," he observed, "and will do very well for our land operations. I am greatly pleased with the harbor site, and it looks so good that I think we should do more and go faster. I would not be a bit surprised if we didn't have a large station here."

Baldwin had already hired test pilot and flight instructor Victor Carlstrom, a former cowpuncher from Wyoming who abandoned a life on the Plains

Mr. Curtiss Comes Calling

This is the first photograph that Frank J. Conway ever took of Curtiss's new flight school and experimental facility at Newport News. Curtiss Aeroplane Company instructor pilots, engineers and ground crew gathered around aircraft that had been rolled out of the station's main hangar on December 29, 1915. A Curtiss flying boat, called an F-boat, is on the left, its tail section resting on a sawhorse. The biplane in the middle is an early version Curtiss JN-2 Jenny, and the biplane in the foreground is a Curtiss JN-4D Jenny. The rear landing gear of the Jenny on the far right, in the foreground, is designed like a ski rather than the more common tail-dragger type. *Courtesy of the author.*

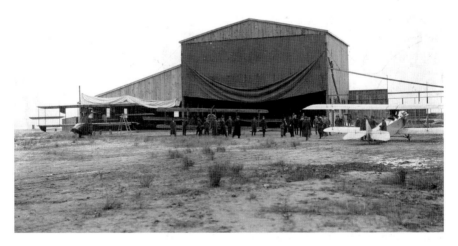

Frank Conway took this picture of the same Curtiss aircraft from a different angle in front of the main hangar. Though Baldwin declared the station "complete" as of December 10, 1915, there was still building going on, and from this picture, taken on December 29, 1915, it is clear this is true. Conway's photograph shows the station on its opening day to the public. *Courtesy of the author.*

Captain Thomas Baldwin's first pilot hires at Newport News were Victor Carlstrom and Walter Edwin Lees. They were also the first two aviators to take aircraft for flights from the station. On the afternoon of December 29, 1915, Carlstrom took off in a Curtiss JN-4D Jenny, the first to do so from the station's landplane field. Lees went up in a Curtiss F-boat. Frank Conway took this and several additional pictures of Carlstrom and Lees that day. This photograph is from Carlstrom's first flight that day. *Courtesy of the author.*

after he saw his first airplane. Before his death at Newport News in the spring of 1917, he held many of the United States' most coveted altitude and endurance records. "Captain Tom" had also hired Walter Edwin Lees, whom he often called his best instructor pilot. "Some men simply never could learn to fly, while others take to it at once," Baldwin observed, talking about Lees. He would later say the same about stage star turned pilot Vernon Castle, who, along with Buck Gallop, became one of the first two Americans to graduate from Baldwin's flight school. "He is a born airman," Baldwin said of Castle, "for he has the touch in his hands. That is essential, and he is one of the most apt pupils I have ever seen."

Carlstrom and Lees were the first two aviators to take airplanes for a flight from Curtiss's station on December 29, 1915, Carlstrom in a Curtiss JN-4D Jenny and Lees in a Curtiss flying boat. Carlstrom and Lees were joined shortly by test pilot and flight instructor Bertrand Blanchard "Bert"

Frank Conway took this wide view of the station on December 29, 1915, so that he could get Carlstrom making a pass over Curtiss's newest facility. Lees's Curtiss F-boat is moored off the end of the seaplane ramp. *Courtesy of the author.*

Acosta, one of the most important figures of early aviation and Rear Admiral Richard Evelyn Byrd's copilot on the admiral's 1927 transatlantic flight, executed two weeks after Charles Lindbergh's famous crossing. There was also Edward Anderson "Eddie" Stinson Jr., a brilliant aircraft designer and wildly popular pilot who signed on to teach budding airmen a thing or two about what their aircraft could do. Stinson was also a world record holder and top-notch stunt flyer. But Baldwin also hired Stewart Wellesley "Andrew" Cogswell, who gave flight lessons to Mary Anita "Neta" Snook, the first woman to take a lesson there and whose later claim to fame was teaching Amelia Earhart to fly. Cogswell later managed the station, put in charge after Captain Baldwin joined the army signal corps during the war. Rounding out the list were Victor Vernon, Carl Truman Batts, Steve MacGordon, Theodore Charles Macaulay, Lawrence Leon, Jimmy Johnson and Theodore Marsh Hequembourg. Hequembourg was a student who graduated from Curtiss's Newport News flight school in early 1916 and

Carpenters were still hard at work on the main hangar under the direction of Randolph Tucker Wood, Baldwin's construction chief and the man seen here standing on the roof in dark coveralls. Though "Captain Tom" declared the station open for business, it was far from complete. Frank Conway took this photograph on December 29, 1915. *Courtesy of the author.*

got a job with Baldwin as an instructor pilot. His brother, Harry Clarence Hequembourg Jr., already worked there as a Curtiss Aeroplane and Motor Company mechanic.

British-born Vernon Castle was a headline everywhere he went. "A born airman" wasn't the first description that came to mind when the public thought of him, not just then. Vernon and Irene Castle were world-famous ballroom dancers who were all the rage from New York City to London. They'd popularized the fox trot and the turkey trot and put their unmistakable stamp on wildly popular cheek-to-cheek dances that left women swooning and their husbands wishing they could dance as well as Vernon. But suddenly and unexpectedly, Vernon had also become a prize pilot. Irene accompanied him to the Virginia Peninsula, and the couple took up residence at Hampton's Chamberlin Hotel. On weekends, they'd take off for theatrical engagements in Washington, D.C., New York City or any major city that booked them to dance. The Castles were the equivalent of modern-day rock stars, making as much as $6,000 a week, an incredible

Mr. Curtiss Comes Calling

Frank Conway took many group photographs during his tenure at the Atlantic Coast Aeronautical Station. This early 1916 photograph has several recognizable faces, including Steve MacGordon, standing up in the Curtiss JN-4D Jenny's cockpit. Standing fourth from the left is Bert Acosta. The man standing third from the right is Harold Marcellus "Buck" Gallop, and next to him on the end of the row are Harry Clarence Hequembourg Jr. and Theodore Marsh Hequembourg. Harry was employed as a Curtiss mechanic before his brother, Ted, became a Curtiss instructor and test pilot. Also tucked in this picture is Charles Terry Wood, kneeling second from the left. Terry was the son of Randolph Tucker Wood, Baldwin's contractor. At the tender age of fifteen, he was the youngest person to ever solo at the station. On the 1920 Census, Terry Wood wrote down his occupation as "avitor [*sic*]." *Courtesy of the author.*

amount of money in 1915. Castle graduated from Curtiss's Newport News flying school in February 1916 but soon departed via New York for the Royal Flying Corps.

Canadians occupied all but two slots in the first class of thirty that started instruction at the station near the end of 1915. The twenty-eight Canadians selected for the class left over one hundred of their countrymen on a wait list. Buck Gallop had to feel lucky about his selection to the first class. He and Castle, who'd become an American citizen before the war, rounded out the group. Luck had little to do with Castle's selection. He paid more than $800 to receive instruction in the first group because he was so anxious to join the Royal Flying Corps and needed to get through the curriculum faster than everyone else. Baldwin required little convincing. Eight hundred

This Curtiss JN-4D Jenny was parked outside the main hangar at the Atlantic Coast Aeronautical Station in early 1916, when this picture was taken. After Curtiss inaugurated the Jenny line in 1915, the army and navy ordered just a small number of the aircraft. Only eleven early model JN-1 and JN-2 aircraft were built. But these were followed quickly by the JN-3, of which fewer than one hundred were made. The JN-4 series that followed introduced the American public to one of the iconic aircraft of the twentieth century. *Courtesy of the Sargeant Memorial Room, Norfolk Public Library.*

Curtiss used the landing gear configuration designed and patented by Grover Loening on the JN-4D aircraft, which eliminated traditional skids and instead put the wheels farther forward with special bracing. These planes also featured wings of unequal spans, with the wingspan greater on the upper wing, the only wing fitted with ailerons. *Courtesy of the Sargeant Memorial Room, Norfolk Public Library.*

This is a cockpit view of the Curtiss JN-4D, photographed in 1916 at the Atlantic Coast Aeronautical Station. The pilot's aeronautical chart is pinned to the instrument console behind the steering column. *Courtesy of the Sargeant Memorial Room, Norfolk Public Library.*

dollars was a considerable sum at that time, and unlike most of the men whose names ended up on the wait list, Castle had the money to pay for what he wanted. At the end of training, each man in the first class received an Aero Club of America certificate that served as the equivalent of a pilot's license. They were not military pilots until accepted by the Royal Flying Corps or the Royal Naval Air Service. Then there was Buck Gallop, a man looking for a purpose.

Buck Gallop was born in Jarvisburg, Currituck County, North Carolina, on March 25, 1895, to Margaret Harrison and Hodges Gallop. His father died when Buck was young, leaving his mother alone to raise him and his brother, also named Hodges. The Gallops moved to Norfolk, Virginia, and from there Buck and Hodges did odd jobs to make ends meet. No one was more grateful than Buck to be accepted into Curtiss's Newport News flying school. He became Baldwin's first American graduate to go to intermediate and advanced training in the army. He'd progressed well in training and would have made his solo flight sooner, but he wanted to take instruction in flying boats as well as landplanes. He got his Aero Club of America certificate in July 1916, well after

By the numbers, a Jenny could only make about seventy-five miles per hour and cruised about ten miles per hour less. It had a landing speed of roughly forty miles per hour. Pilots complained that it handled sluggishly and had a nonexistent rate of climb at two hundred feet per minute. Recovering from a stall wasn't easy and ate up valuable altitude. The Jenny's OX-5 engine often ran rough and was unreliable, thus about 20 percent of all JN-4Ds built were lost during flight training. This close-up view of the Jenny's OX-5 engine was also taken in 1916 in Newport News. *Courtesy of the Sargeant Memorial Room, Norfolk Public Library.*

the men he'd started training with at the first of the year. By graduation, Gallop had decided he would take what he learned into combat, something he hadn't figured out when he first signed up for flight instruction. After graduation, he was accepted into the United States Army Signal Corps Aviation Section and later commanded the Ninetieth Aero Squadron in France. He also held L'Escadrille Lafayette certificate number two.

Gallop lived the life of which legends are made. As a combat pilot in France, he was busted more than once for flying after he'd been grounded. Colorful and unconventional, he was the war's most successful hell-raiser. Despite his penchant for trouble, Gallop was much loved by the public. They saw him as a war hero who lived big and played hard. After the war, he continued the adventure and barnstormed the United States with a flying circus. But he tired of it after crisscrossing the country one too many times. He became a

While there was no name to go with this aviator, Frank Conway took the picture in late 1916 at the Atlantic Coast Aeronautical Station. The aircraft is the Curtiss JN-4D Jenny. *Courtesy of the author.*

soldier of fortune before World War II, offering his flying services to a Chinese warlord. Gallop became the subject of a book titled *The Silver Bullet*, which got its title from Gallop's misfortune. His "silver bullet" adventure left Gallop lucky to be alive. Part of his stomach was shot away, leaving him unable to consume more than small portions of food at one time.

Done by the book, flight instruction in the Jenny was completed in about fifty hours over the course of six to eight weeks. Training began in the front seat, with between four to ten hours of dual seat instruction. Curtiss's instructors didn't always follow this seating arrangement. But regardless of where the instructor sat, he had to scream directions to his student over the roar of the aircraft's engine. Soloing moved the student into the backseat. The Jenny was always, without exception, soloed from the back. After twenty-four hours of flying solo, followed by sixteen hours cross-country, training was complete. Wartime circumstances accelerated this process. Stage star Vernon Castle was photographed in the front seat of the Curtiss JN-4D at Newport News. Instructor Bert Acosta is in the rear cockpit. Castle graduated in February 1916. *Courtesy of the Library of Congress Prints and Photographs Division.*

Hollywood didn't forget Gallop either. His exploits in France were the subject of the 1930 movie *Dawn Patrol*, starring Richard Barthelmess as Gallop, Douglas Fairbanks Jr. and Neil Hamilton. The screenplay was based on the story by John Monk Saunders, who had served in the air service during the war but was never posted to France; he took home an Oscar for his work on the film. Saunders also wrote the screenplays for *Wings* in 1927; *The Last Flight*, adapted from his novel *Single Lady*, in 1931; and *The Conquest of the Air*, a 1936 picture he also directed.

Gallop's personal life was tumultuous. He married Newport News native Maxine Finch while still in flight school, but they divorced. After *Dawn Patrol* popularized his life, Gallop went to work in 1931 for a New York advertising

Above: Atlantic Coast Aeronautical Station Building No. 5 was photographed by Frank Conway in the spring of 1916. This one-story cottage on the water was built for the recreation and relaxation of Baldwin's flight instructors, test pilots and visitors to the Atlantic Coast Aeronautical Station. *Courtesy of the author.*

Right: Frank Conway photographed Captain Tom Baldwin, Atlantic Coast Aeronautical Station administrator, in early 1916. Baldwin had more than forty years of aeronautical experience, primarily as an aeronaut who'd started designing and building aircraft late in his life. Baldwin had an international reputation before he accepted Curtiss's offer to run his Newport News operation. *Courtesy of the author.*

Curtiss Flying School instructors, test pilots, plane crews and students gathered with Captain Thomas Scott Baldwin in the winter of 1916 for this picture by Frank Conway. Baldwin is standing second from left. Others notable in the photograph are Jimmy Johnson (kneeling, third from left), Major Billy Mitchell's primary instructor pilot; Walter Edwin Lees (kneeling, fourth from left), who sent Mitchell aloft on his first solo; Carl Truman Batts (left center, with arm raised); Theodore "Ted" Hequembourg (standing, fifth from right), also called "Dore" by his flight students; Bertrand Blanchard "Bert" Acosta (on aircraft, left); Steve MacGordon (on aircraft, center); and Stewart Wellesley "Andrew" Cogswell (on aircraft, right), the instructor who taught Neta Snook, Amelia Earhart's future flying instructor, to fly. *Courtesy of the author.*

firm that managed the Jergens hand lotion account. He married Amy Branch Jergens, former wife of Andrew Nicholas Jergens and an heir in her divorce settlement to the company fortune. The wedding took place in Virginia Beach, Virginia, on April 25, 1940. Gallop died on April 9, 1943.

Back at the aeronautical station, it was Saturday, January 2, 1916, and the station had only been open to the public for three days. But on that day, there were so many people trying to get down to the municipal small boat harbor to watch Baldwin's pilots demonstrate Curtiss aircraft that John B. Megginson, superintendent of the Newport News and Hampton Railway, Gas and Electric Company, announced a fifteen-minute trolley car schedule from the shipyard to the municipal small boat harbor "today and tomorrow

Curtiss's Newport News facility was in the business of developing new aircraft, and this involved extensive aircraft experimentation and flight test. An aircraft seen one day might be gone the next, its airframe and engines parted out and used on another work in progress. Curtiss established the Atlantic Coast Aeronautical Station to test his hydroaeroplanes in warmer water. He couldn't do this at Hammondsport and Buffalo. Water froze over in winter months. Before Curtiss was able to contract the site in Newport News, he returned to Norfolk waters, well suited to hydroaeroplane testing, to work on a new project. This aircraft, photographed at the foot of the docks leading up to the old marine hospital in Norfolk's Berkley section probably about 1915, was a Curtiss floatplane experiment and a one-off. Curtiss mechanics towed the aircraft to this location on a small barge. While it is fitted with floats, the aircraft is incomplete. There is no motor installed. *Courtesy of the Sargeant Memorial Room, Norfolk Public Library.*

in order that everyone may have the opportunity to witness the flights." The *Daily Press* that morning reported that several members of the school's first class had, the day before, made flights of fifteen minutes' duration. "Flights will be made throughout the day today and tomorrow, there will be no holiday for the students, several of whom will leave in a few weeks for Europe to join the aviation corps of the allied armies of Europe." One week later, the newspaper reported important news pertaining to the flying field when it ran the following:

> *The Curtiss Aeroplane Company yesterday secured from the Old Dominion Land Company and T.C. Powell, the privilege to build, maintain and use a speedway for testing high powered aeroplanes on a course extending from*

An early version of the Curtiss F-boat met an unfortunate end in the water just off the aeronautical station's beach in the spring of 1916. Baldwin's aeronautical engineers and mechanics were photographed by Frank Conway trying to salvage the aircraft using a towline attached to a horse on the shore, just out of view. *Courtesy of the author.*

The men in this photograph kept Captain Tom's aircraft flying. From left, Percy Platt Kirkham, Bill Day, Stanley Irving Vaughn and James "Jimmy" Honor were photographed in early 1916 in front of Curtiss JN-4D Jenny. Percy Kirkham was Baldwin's chief aircraft engineer and mechanic and brother of Curtiss's chief engine designer, Charles Kirkham. Vaughn, also a pilot, continued to work for Curtiss as his Buffalo factory manager after leaving Newport News. Jimmy Honor came to the United States from his native Middlesex, England, to work as a mechanic for the Curtiss Aeroplane Company. He was gone from Newport News before it closed in 1922. *Courtesy of the author.*

Walter Edwin Lees (standing at left) came to Newport News at the end of 1915 and joined Victor Carlstrom as one of Captain Baldwin's first two flight instructors and test pilots. Carlstrom and Lees would soon be joined by Victor Vernon, Steve MacGordon, Theodore Marsh "Ted" Hequembourg, Harry Clarence Hequembourg Jr., Lawrence Leon, Carl Truman Batts, James Mussey "Jimmy" Johnson, Bertrand Blanchard "Bert" Acosta and Stewart Wellesley "Andrew" Cogswell (shown at right). The photograph was taken by Frank J. Conway in early 1916. Lees and Cogswell are standing in front of a Curtiss JN-4D Jenny. *Courtesy of the author.*

Salter's Creek to Ivy Avenue. It is reported from an authoritative source that the aeroplane company will test out here, all or a great part of the 1,500 machines ordered by one of the great entente powers of Europe. The speedway is to be between 50 and 100 feet wide and the earth will be leveled, packed and rolled. The high powered machines in question will attain a speed of 140 miles per hour. It was also stated that the aeroplane people have secured 10 acres of land on Salter's Creek for the assembling, testing and housing a part of the machines. The plat will give the company a base at either end of the course, one on Salter's Creek and the other at the municipal small boat harbor.

The British had just placed an order for over $1 million in aircraft from the Curtiss Aeroplane and Motor Company.

Soon after its first busy weekend, Curtiss instructor pilot Charles McHenry Pond transferred from Buffalo to Newport News to move more students through basic flight instruction. Pond, the son of Rear Admiral Charles Fremont Pond, was considered one of the foremost aviators of his day. He

Walter Lees shared his love of flying with his wife, the former Loa Catherine Lloyd, after their June 17, 1915 marriage. She flew with him as often as his schedule allowed and until her first pregnancy precluded it. After their first child was born, Loa resumed flying as Walter's passenger. The couple arrived in Newport News, Virginia, on December 19, 1915, for Lees to begin his new job as flight instructor and test pilot for the Curtiss Aeroplane and Motor Company. Lees had just taken Loa up in a Curtiss F-boat when this picture was taken in 1916. *Courtesy of the author.*

was followed from Buffalo by another, Steve MacGordon, who reported a week later. MacGordon held the world record for looping the loop, his record being twenty-one loops in eighteen minutes. But MacGordon's arrival was back-page news to Vernon Castle. On the morning of January 22, 1916, the *Daily Press* carried an interesting piece that read:

> *Vernon Castle, dancer and aeronautical student, yesterday was summoned to appear in the police court this morning on a charge of exceeding the speed limit with his automobile. Patrolman Smith, who is responsible for his predicament, avers that the dancer was rushing down Jefferson Avenue to the municipal small boat harbor in a racing car [a 1914 Mercer] at a speed something like 30 miles an hour.*

This wasn't Castle's first speeding ticket with the Mercer, and it was certainly not his last. Castle made the drive from the Chamberlin Hotel to the airfield in that car, and he was normally not alone. He had many lady

Frank Conway took this picture of Charlotte Jane Kennan Lloyd, Loa's mother, with granddaughter Loa Betty Lees, probably in early spring 1917. Josephine "Jo" Cooper, Lees's biographer and daughter, recalled later that her older sisters—Loa Betty, Aerial Burt and Charlotte Jane, whom they nicknamed "Billie"—affectionately called their grandmother "Danny" rather than "Granny." *Courtesy of the author.*

admirers who rode with him back and forth, a fan club that every so often landed him in hot water with Irene.

The aeronautical station was in business just over a month when, on January 26, 1916, Baldwin permitted Walter Lees to take visitors for rides in his Curtiss flying boat. The objective was to acclimate the public firsthand to aircraft. The following morning, Vernon Castle brought budding stage actress Pinna Nesbitt over to the station for a ride with Lees. She was known largely for her appearances in melodramas directed by her then-husband Harley Knoles and released in 1917 and 1918. "Come on" rides were also a way to generate public interest in enrolling to take flight instruction. This was an expensive proposition. The Curtiss Aeroplane and Motor Company fixed the cost for flight instruction at $1 per minute. Flight instruction took four hundred minutes in a landplane. Seaplane instruction took just as long and was charged at the same rate. But there was a combined course for both aircraft types offered for $600. Most flights were brief. Curtiss's flight instructors could teach six to ten students from one class and averaged

Loa Betty Lees, baby daughter of Curtiss instructor pilot Walter Lees, was photographed at the Atlantic Coast Aeronautical Station in early 1917 by Frank Conway. Born at Buxton Hospital, now part of Mary Immaculate Hospital, on March 9, 1916, Betty was a playful, happy child and obviously a favorite subject of photographer Conway. *Courtesy of the author.*

roughly ten flights a day. Walter Lees was busy. Between teaching students and giving public rides, he was flying every day of the week and on Saturdays and Sundays.

The following day, January 28, Lees flew into the limelight as a lifesaver when a local man named Arthur Johnson capsized his Old Town canoe one thousand feet from shore. Lees took off in his flying boat after Johnson. Johnson was in no danger of drowning, but there was no one else to fetch him back to land other than a "bird boat." But there was more excitement that day, too. Stewart Cogswell walked into the arc of a flying boat's whirring propeller and badly cut his left arm.

Most of the people Lees took up in his flying boat didn't articulate the experience like Richmond businessman George Henry Black, who came to Newport News to have a look at the flying school and hoped to get a ride. When a Richmond reporter asked him how the flight felt, Black's comments made his hometown paper and the *Daily Press*:

Mr. Curtiss Comes Calling

Curtiss's Newport News station was visited on April 8, 1916, by a delegation from the Aero Club of America that included President Alan Ramsey Hawley; Rear Admiral Robert E. Peary, renowned polar explorer; Professor David Peck Todd, well-known astronomer; Henry Woodhouse, club governor and director of the American Society of Aeronautic Engineers; George Douglas Wardrop, editor of *Aerial Age* and former assistant secretary to Theodore Roosevelt; and Edward V. "Turk Bird" Gardner, club member and later a United States army aeronautic instructor and United States airmail pilot. Several members of this delegation were photographed by Frank Conway during the visit. Pictured from left to right are Woodhouse, Wardrop, Glenn Curtiss, unidentified man, Todd, unidentified man, Hawley, Baldwin and another unidentified man. Gardner was the nation's second airmail pilot, making some of the most historic flights in history in this capacity, including the first Pathfinder flights that led to future transcontinental airmail delivery. He was killed while stunt flying at a Kansas county fair in 1920. *Courtesy of the author.*

Well, it's a great sport. You feel when you begin to rise that every care has left you, and the higher you go the lighter you feel, and the sensation is as if you had wings and were really flying yourself. You never think of the distance you are up. It is like being on a very high peak overlooking a valley. The houses and other buildings look small and the air you breathe makes you feel buoyant.

Black could feel the Chesapeake Bay's cool air wafting over him as Lees's flying boat rose high over the earth and sea. When they touched down on the water, it was warm, and spray from the plane's wake kicked gently along its hull.

Rear Admiral Robert Edwin Peary, American naval officer and arctic explorer, is shown here about 1909 standing on the main deck of the steamship *Roosevelt* wearing his arctic cold weather gear. Peary was a frequent visitor to the Atlantic Coast Aeronautical Station, making several trips beyond his participation in the April 8, 1916 Aero Club of America visit. Peary spent his final years as a champion of aviation and military readiness and chaired the National Aero Coast Patrol Commission. He died on February 20, 1920, in Washington, D.C. *Courtesy of the Library of Congress Prints and Photographs Division.*

A Curtiss F-boat was parked outside the United States House of Representatives Building in Washington, D.C., at the behest of Rear Admiral Peary's National Aero Coast Patrol Commission. The placard next to the aircraft opined that Russia already had eighty F-boats protecting its territorial waters, and "we have none." Less than two months after his visit to Curtiss's Newport News facility, Peary outlined an aero coast defense system comprising a coast patrol or picket line of sentinel seaplanes operating fifty to one hundred miles offshore and a series of squadron stations each equipped to handle a few hundred fighting seaplanes. The stations, he argued, should be collocated with larger coast cities and sea gateways. *Courtesy of the Library of Congress Prints and Photographs Division.*

The day after Black's ride, six Canadians and Vernon Castle were scheduled to take their final flight test. Each man would have to complete ten figure eights, one successful dead-stick landing from an altitude of 1,000 feet and landing within 150 feet of a preselected site. (A dead-stick landing is executed without the benefit of the airplane's engine running.) Castle wasted no time letting his classmates know he'd see them in England when they got done. Despite his bravado, Castle was what Baldwin said he was: a natural-born pilot. The six Canadians finished their tests without a hitch, and Castle, after all his talk, postponed until he and Irene returned from New York City, where they fulfilled a farewell dancing engagement at the Hippodrome.

Castle graduated on February 5. But so did Canadians Frederick Charles Biette, Arthur Trelvar Whealey and Charles Leonard Bailey, all of Toronto, Canada. The Canadians' Royal Aero Club aviator certificates document their graduation on this date from the "Atlantic Coast Aeronautic School."

A Curtiss Twin JN—often called a Model 1B, a JN-4 Twin Tractor, a JN-5 and a Curtiss Buffalo—was also put on display outside the House congressional building by Peary's commission. The one-off biplane trainer variant of this aircraft was tested at Newport News on August 21, 1916. Victor Carlstrom was its test pilot. This experimental observation aircraft was produced for further military testing as an enlarged single-seat, twin-engine version of the Curtiss JN-4D Jenny. The aircraft was powered by two Curtiss OXX-2 water-cooled V-8 piston engines. To demonstrate the versatility of the aircraft for lawmakers, it was fitted out in its landplane and seaplane configuration. Only eight Twin JNs were built for the United States Army Signal Corps Air Service, one of which was evaluated by the navy as a twin-float seaplane. *Courtesy of the Library of Congress Prints and Photographs Division.*

Canadian John Foster Chisholm, of Quebec, graduated on February 19, 1916. Harry Saxon Pell, also of Toronto, graduated on March 18, 1916, and was killed in action on April 6, 1917, the day the United States entered the war. Most of the Canadian flyers who trained at the Atlantic Coast Aeronautical Station and other American and foreign flight schools of this period, with few exceptions, can be located through their Royal Aero Club registrations.

Curtiss's Atlantic Coast Aeronautical Station competed with the Castles for media in its first two months in business. But in the first week of February 1916, Baldwin's pilots and planes knocked the Castles off the marquee when William Randolph Hearst's newsreel outfit, International Film Company, sent J.P. Gillette to Newport News to take moving pictures of the flying field for distribution to movie theaters across the country. In total, Gillette shot a five-hundred-foot reel of film of the Atlantic Coast Aeronautical Station.

Mr. Curtiss Comes Calling

Commander Holden Chester Richardson, Naval Aviator No. 13 and the navy's chief aviation constructor, was the senior member of the board present at Newport News on August 21, 1916, for the Curtiss Twin JN flight test. Richardson was the navy's first engineering test pilot, pioneer designer of flying boat hulls and catapults, codesigner of the Navy/Curtiss flying boat and pilot of the NC-3 on its May 1919 transatlantic attempt. Vice Admiral Patrick Neison Lynch Bellinger, Naval Aviator No. 8, later said that Richardson did more for naval aviation and got less credit for it than anyone he'd ever known. *Courtesy of the George Grantham Bain Collection, Library of Congress Prints and Photographs Division.*

After the hoopla generated by Hearst's film crew, the February 6 *Daily Press* reported that Glenn Curtiss and his family were due to arrive that afternoon at the Chamberlin Hotel, where they would remain for ten days. "Mr. Curtiss," the newspaper noted, "is coming here to be near the school and at the same time take a short vacation." The newspaper also reported that Curtiss wanted more land at the boat harbor. Curtiss visited Newport News several times, alone and with his family, during the height of the station's two-year civilian flight school program, which did not include the training period set aside for United States Navy and Army student pilots who began training there in the spring of 1917.

Curtiss had just gone back home when, on February 17, 1916, the aeronautical station was visited by Imperial Russian Air Service Lieutenant Commander Victor Victorovich Utgoff and a representative of his government. They came to Newport News to observe three kinds of aircraft being used to train flight students. Utgoff commented that he believed many of Curtiss's current aircraft, as well as those that he would produce in the future, would be tested at Newport News. The following day, Victor Carlstrom set a station record when he took a Curtiss JN-4D Jenny up to nine thousand feet. Despite the fact that it took him a half hour to reach that altitude, Utgoff, who observed the flight from the

Just two days after the Aero Club of America's Newport News visit on April 10, 1916, Curtiss flight instructor and test pilot Steve MacGordon, accompanied by a Canadian flight student, set a new American altitude record for an airplane carrying a passenger when MacGordon soared to 14,800 feet in a Curtiss military tractor-biplane. MacGordon broke the record previously held by Army Lieutenant Joseph E. Carberry at San Diego, California, when he went to 11,690 feet on January 5, 1915. Carberry is pictured in 1913, the same year he and twenty-three other army men were chosen to be military aviators. *Courtesy of the Library of Congress Prints and Photographs Division*

ground, came away impressed. An aviation writer for the *Daily Press* wrote the next day:

> *The machine circled slowly up into the air, mounting gradually and so steadily that there apparently was not the slightest lost motion. Higher and higher went the daring pilot. The watching thousands expected him to turn back at any minute and were breathless with surprise when the machine finally disappeared in the clouds.*

Utgoff eventually rose to second in command of the Imperial Russian Air Service, and after the October 1917 revolution that toppled Czar Nicholas II and the Romanov dynasty, he came to the United States to stay, relocating to New York, where he bought a chicken farm on which his old friend Igor Sikorsky built his first aircraft factory. Utgoff enlisted in the United States Coast Guard in 1929, making flights out of Gloucester, Massachusetts. He was killed in a private aircraft crash in 1930.

Vernon Castle stayed in the news. But not all the ink he got made Irene happy. The February 20, 1916 *New York Journal* reported his departure for England with a few details that would have been better left out:

Mr. Curtiss Comes Calling

Frank J. Conway photographed Vernon Castle, briefly an instructor pilot at Curtiss's Newport News flying school after completion of his own flight training there on February 5, 1916. Photographs of Castle during his association with Curtiss's Peninsula airfield are rare. Those outside Conway who tried to snap his picture were almost always told no. When asked why, he would tell the disappointed photographer that he was paid to have his picture taken. *Courtesy of the author.*

Speeded by the cheers and tears of hundreds of his friends, Vernon Castle, the dancer, today is on his way to England. He boarded the White Star Liner Adriatic *amid a tumultuous waving of flags. Just as the gangplank was about to be drawn up, a handsome and fashionably-clad young woman brushed her way through the crowd. She practically fought her way to the dancer's side. Then she threw her arms around him. Five times, onlookers say, she kissed him. Castle blushed profusely.*

So where, the public wondered, was Mrs. Castle when all the hugging and kissing was going on? Irene Castle was in Saint Louis, Missouri, on business, where Vernon had left her before making his way to New York City to board the *Adriatic*. When she got hold of the *New York Journal* article and saw pictures of her husband being smothered with kisses by the gangplank crasher, Vernon's next word from Irene came in the form of a "burning letter" to England. She left off her customary love and kisses.

A Curtiss Aeroplane Company "Bat" boat, a floatplane, was nicknamed for its unique wing shape and short hull. The Bat boat was designed by Glenn Curtiss for the United States Navy. The aircraft was tested at Curtiss's Newport News airfield, where this picture was taken about 1916. Though it was generally considered a successful design, the navy didn't order the aircraft, thus it never got beyond prototype. *Courtesy of the Hampton Roads Naval Museum.*

Curtiss's Newport News station was watched closely by aviation advocates in the United States Congress. Arkansas Democrat Senator Joseph Taylor Robinson charged that the army signal corps aviation section was woefully equipped and "contemptibly inefficient." Robinson blamed the army's problem on deficient aircraft and poor training syllabi. He waited for the War Department to investigate. It didn't. In the meantime, poorly prepared army flyers had been killed in flawed aircraft. The army, he observed, couldn't properly train its own men to fly aircraft. Robinson didn't trust the War Department to manage the inquiry either. He believed the investigation had to be conducted outside the army.

The navy had problems as serious as those experienced by the army. Public debate over the contemptible state of military aviation pushed more American and foreign students into Curtiss's flight schools. His Newport News school received successive groups of students in the spring of 1916 that continued to include a large number of Canadians, including Harold Drummond, who graduated on April 4, 1916, and Everett Maitland Smith, who graduated on May 2, 1916. Drummond and Smith were from Toronto. By the arrival of

George Eustace Amyot Hallett, photographed by Frank Conway in 1916 at Newport News, Virginia, first met Glenn Curtiss when Curtiss was in San Diego, California, in late 1910 to conduct hydroaeroplane experiments that couldn't be done in Hammondsport, New York, on Lake Keuka because it froze over in the winter. Curtiss rented a powerboat from the Baker Machine Shop, where Hallett was foreman. Hallett was brought from San Diego to Hammondsport to work on the *America* and also on the development of a navy hydroaeroplane. In addition to being a master machinist, Curtiss put Hallett through flight training. He was certified as a pilot. When Hallett filled out his World War I draft registration, he listed his employer as the United States War Department, North Island, San Diego. Hallett had been commissioned a major in the United States Army Air Service and assigned as chief of the Power Plant Section, Engineering Division, Air Service, Dayton, Ohio. Hallett, arguably one of the most important Curtiss cohorts, was born in Cheltenham, England, on May 9, 1890, and died on June 2, 1982, in San Diego. *Courtesy of the author.*

the second class, Baldwin warned flight instructors and incoming students that the absence of accidents in the first months of the school's operation was due to an overabundance of caution. Baldwin didn't send an aircraft up unless it was in excellent working condition. He also grounded aircraft in poor weather. Curtiss and Baldwin promoted flight safety to minimize accidents and instill public confidence in the operation of aircraft.

By the middle of March 1916, Baldwin proudly announced that as the result of Imperial Russian Air Service Lieutenant Commander Utgoff's visit, Russia bought $4 million in aircraft from the Curtiss Aeroplane and Motor Company. Curtiss turned an enormous profit as war raged in Europe. Certainly, Curtiss's Newport News test pilots, led by Victor Carlstrom, played a significant role in the sale to Russia. Baldwin had numerous Curtiss JN-4D Jenny aircraft, Curtiss F-boats and, at any given time, a diverse selection of experimental aircraft waiting to be tested. Newspapers reported what they could see on the airfield and in the water. They were quick to notice when five scout planes showed up, accompanied by six mechanics from Buffalo to assemble them for flight test. They also noticed when a "giant flying boat" arrived and was being put together in a hangar specially built to keep it through assembly and testing. The experimental flying boat was described as a two-engine, 360-horsepower aircraft capable of carrying four to five men and "one of the largest of its kind in existence." With such aircraft at his disposal, Victor Carlstrom, Curtiss's chief test pilot, flew speed and endurance flights between Newport News and Fisherman's Island at Cape Charles in 1916 using a twin-engine Curtiss hydroconvertible land and seaplane. Carlstrom's record-breaking speed test at Newport News was acclaimed by the Aero Club of America as "the most important aviation event of the year." The result for Curtiss was worldwide recognition, the aircraft sale to Russia and an additional $3 million sale to England.

But Carlstrom wasn't the only one making news. On March 24, 1916, Pilot Charles Gordon took an R-2 aircraft up to 14,000 feet, breaking Carlstrom's earlier record of 9,000 feet in a JN-4D and also an earlier record set by Navy Lieutenant (junior grade) Saufley, Naval Aviator No. 14, who took a Curtiss AH-15 to 11,056 feet on November 30, 1915, and reached 11,975 feet in the AH-14 on December 3, 1915. Gordon was airborne three hours and forty-five minutes, until extreme cold forced him to land. Captain Baldwin, who didn't know any better at the time, associated Gordon's experience with extreme cold with the time of year rather than high altitude and remarked widely to reporters that he intended for his most experienced pilots to go after the world altitude record as soon as the weather "warmed up."

Gordon's record was short-lived. Lieutenant (junior grade) Saufley broke Gordon's record on March 29 when he took an AH-14 to 16,010 feet and surpassed this altitude on April 2 by going to 16,072 feet in the same aircraft. Saufley also broke a seaplane endurance record by staying aloft in the AH-9 at Pensacola, Florida, for eight hours, forty-three minutes, on June 4, 1916, a record he shattered five days later by remaining in the air for eight hours, fifty-one minutes. But it was the last record he would ever break. Saufley died in the line of duty in the AH-9 just eight minutes after breaking his previous record, crashing to his death at one o'clock in the afternoon in a nosedive from 700 feet above Santa Rosa Island. Saufley's accident was attributed to a structural flaw in the tail surfaces of the AH-9 and triggered an investigation that underscored the unsatisfactory nature of aircraft then in use. Senator Robinson's earlier concern was affirmed by Saufley's death, which brought to a halt all training at Pensacola until the first Curtiss N-9s were delivered on November 26, 1916.

2

THOSE DARING YOUNG MEN AND THEIR FLYING MACHINES

G lenn Curtiss returned to Newport News on April 3, 1916. His visit was cause for celebration, but the day didn't start out that way. Instructor pilot Stewart Cogswell and British-born mechanic James "Jimmy" Honor crashed a flying boat headlong into Hampton Roads. They demolished the aircraft but weren't seriously hurt. Curtiss wasn't pleased when he heard the news. Two days later, Captain Frederick Daniel Cock, president of the Newport News chapter of the Navy League of the United States and a harbor pilot employed by the Virginia Pilots Association, announced in the April 5, 1916 *Daily Press* that he was going to fly to Washington, D.C., aboard one of the Curtiss flying school's aircraft—which one, he did not know. Cock's mission was to convey to the Wilson White House that the mayors of Virginia's Peninsula cities were unsatisfied with the president's war preparedness policy. "The trip will be made in a large flying boat," said Cock, "but may be made in a landplane if it is decided to land on one of the White House parks. Mr. Curtiss stated he intends to give aviation all the publicity he can from now on as he believes it will educate the public to the need for more adequate aerial defense."

Curtiss was convinced that flight instructor and test pilot Steve MacGordon's flight carrying Cock to Washington via airplane would clearly demonstrate that even the nation's capital wasn't safe from hostile aircraft attack in times of war. The United States had few modern aircraft, and the old ones were, in Curtiss's opinion, unable to "cope with machines now being used by European belligerents. Machines from a hostile fleet on the Atlantic coast could bomb the nation's capital with ease." Alan Ramsey Hawley, then president of the Aero Club of America, reiterated Curtiss's point when he sent a letter to United States Congressman Charles Lieb urging the congressman to push for establishment of a department of aeronautics and a presidential cabinet secretary tasked only with the

Curtiss flight instructor and test pilot Steve MacGordon set a new cross-country record on his flight from Newport News, Virginia, to Washington, D.C., on April 1, 1916. His passenger on the flight was British Royal Naval Service Lieutenant Vivian Hewett, in the United States to inspect aircraft for the British government and a resident at the Atlantic Coast Aeronautical Station for several weeks in early 1916. Hewett is sitting in the first row of this picture, fourth from the right, nearly at center. Kneeling directly behind Hewett on the left is Stewart Cogswell, and to the right is Steve MacGordon. Captain Thomas Baldwin is standing directly behind MacGordon. He is the man in the dark suit, bow tie and fedora. Standing in the front row, third from the right in the dark turtleneck, is Curtiss test pilot Theodore Charles Macaulay. *Courtesy of the author.*

development of aeronautics for military use. Hawley observed a need for a national air service of no fewer than five thousand aircraft. "With five thousand aeroplanes," he wrote, "this country would be placed in the safe position of a porcupine, which goes about its daily peaceful pursuits, harms no one, but is ever ready to defend itself." Curtiss opined that the country had so few aircraft in its inventory to defend the nation's coastline, let alone its capital, that he'd favor educating the public about the aerial unpreparedness of the United States. Recognizing the inherent value of having Curtiss's operation on its doorstep, the Newport News Common Council granted the aeronautical station a twenty-year lease on April 11, 1916, on the site of the municipal small boat harbor, thus knocking Norfolk out of the running to draw Curtiss's aeronautical station and his Buffalo manufacturing plant to the former Jamestown Exposition grounds.

Those Daring Young Men and Their Flying Machines

Born on July 11, 1893, in Fort Payne, Alabama, Edward "Eddie" Anderson Stinson Jr. left home at age sixteen to fly airplanes. This barnstormer, stunt pilot and record-setting aviator was schooled by the Wright brothers and, in 1917, took up residence in Newport News, Virginia, as an instructor pilot at Glenn Curtiss's Atlantic Coast Aeronautical Station. This Frank Conway photograph was taken at Newport News during the peak of Stinson's tenure as flight instructor and test pilot. Stinson set several world records at Newport News. During World War I, he held a lieutenant's commission in the United States Army Air Service. In 1920, nine years after he learned to fly, Stinson founded the Stinson Aircraft Company in Dayton, Ohio. Five years later, in 1925, Stinson made Detroit, Michigan, the base of operations for his company. Over the next three decades, more than thirteen thousand aircraft would carry the Stinson brand. Eddie Stinson did not live to enjoy the success of his company. He died in an air crash in Chicago on January 26, 1932. At the time of his death at age thirty-eight, he had logged more than sixteen thousand hours of flight time, more than any other pilot to date. *Courtesy of the author.*

By the second week of April 1916, the Atlantic Coast Aeronautical Station took delivery of this Sturtevant biplane. The Sturtevant was the first aircraft to have an all-metal fuselage. The Sturtevant Aeroplane Company, in business from 1915 to 1918, was formed by its parent company, B.F. Sturtevant Company, to develop military aircraft. The new company was based at Jamaica Plain, Massachusetts. The company produced a number of aircraft for both the army and the navy, popularly called the Battle S4 airplane of naval type. The United States Navy bought twelve of the S-design, all metal and highly innovative for aircraft of that period; the army bought four; and the Rhode Island Militia, one. These seventeen aircraft are recognized as the first all-metal aircraft used by the United States military. The aircraft shown here was designed by Grover Loening, Sturtevant's chief designer. It is the Model A battle plane finished in 1915 and sent to Newport News for flight test. This is a one-of-a-kind experimental fighter. *Courtesy of the Sargeant Memorial Room, Norfolk Public Library.*

Soon after Curtiss's statement went public, the Aero Club of America created the National Aeroplane Fund to be used to train civilian and American military student aviators at Curtiss's Newport News aeronautical station. Up to that time, the vast majority of men who came there to train were civilian. But in April 1916 that changed. National guardsmen and signal corps reservists began showing up in large numbers, and so did prospective army and navy pilots. Curtiss's company already provided free training to militia officers from seventeen states, detailed to Newport News by their adjutant generals. Then, on September 6, 1916, the army announced that Newport News would serve as the principal training station for its military aviators. By the war's end, a statistic worth repeating, more than one thousand army aviators graduated from Curtiss's Newport News flying school, and even this number is dwarfed by the total number of foreign and American flyers trained there before the United States declared war a year later.

On April 8, 1916, the aeronautical station received an Aero Club of America delegation led by Hawley that included Rear Admiral Robert Edwin Peary, America's renowned polar explorer; Professor David Peck Todd, an astronomer and aviation advocate; Henry Woodhouse, club governor and director of the American Society of Aeronautic Engineers; George Douglas Wardrop, editor of *Aerial Age* and former assistant secretary to Theodore Roosevelt; and Edward V. "Turk Bird" Gardner, club member and later a United States army aeronautic instructor and United States airmail pilot. Hawley's presence at Newport News was testament to the station's importance on the aviation scene.

Though they arrived in the worst of weather, members of the club took several short flights. The object of their visit was summed up during a press conference at the Warwick Hotel when a spokesman told reporters:

> *A committee from the Aero Club of America arrived at Newport News this morning to take stock of the militia officers and civilian aviators who are learning to fly, to see how many men could be made available to form an aero corps to meet an emergency in connection with the Mexican campaign.*

The committee met with more than forty militia officers and civilian aviators who were then in flight training or waiting for their turn to come up. At that time, there were between ten and twelve aircraft set aside for training purposes, an insufficient number to push all the men on the school's wait list. After the Aero Club evaluation, additional aircraft and equipment were delivered from Curtiss's Buffalo plant.

The Aero Club committee did marvel at some of Curtiss's larger aircraft, but most especially the huge flying boat *America*, built for Rodman Wanamaker's planned transatlantic flight that year, which first flew on June 23, 1914. Though he paid Curtiss $25,000 to build it, any plan to cross the Atlantic was cancelled once the war in Europe started. With the exception of it being smaller, the *America* was the template for Curtiss's larger flying boats then under construction for the American and British navies. Club members were told that Curtiss and Baldwin intended to assemble the *America* at Newport News, but it couldn't be test flown while they were there

April 1916 saw the arrival of a mysterious figure who had already made national headlines for his marriage to the wealthy widow of James Henry "Silent" Smith—Annie Armstrong Stewart Smith. Jean Harold Edward Saint Cyr was living the high life. He drove a foreign-make touring car that came with a liveried footman and a chauffeur. He told reporters that he was tired of yachting and hoped to find greater pleasure in flying. He had come to Newport News to fly. But there was something about Saint Cyr that wasn't quite right. A series of articles in the February 1916 *New York World* reported that he was living a dual life and that he was really a missing man named Jack Thompson from Waco, Texas. Thompson was a poor man who had vanished, only to resurface as millionaire devil-may-care Saint Cyr. He is shown here, standing in the doorway, in this undated period photograph. *Courtesy of the George Grantham Bain Collection, Library of Congress Prints and Photographs Division.*

due to many missing parts. The *America* also required a specially constructed derrick to put it in the water. Wanamaker's flying boat had a wingspan of seventy-two feet and was originally fitted with two ninety-horsepower OX-5 V-8 engines. The *America* was the largest flying boat ever built in the United States up to that time, but it would soon be bested by bigger and faster Curtiss flying boats, including a triplane flying boat for Wanamaker, also originally scheduled to be assembled at Newport News.

The *America* was similar to flying boats then under development in Europe. But one Aero Club member opined, having observed what Curtiss's station had to offer, that in case of trouble, "our navy would be just as badly off as the army is today. The navy would not have sufficient aeroplanes to last one week." The committee noted, too, that Curtiss's Atlantic Coast Aeronautical Station had more equipment on hand than either the army or navy, and it was the committee's opinion that there ought to be no fewer than twelve similar aeronautical stations in the United States under federal control, six for the army and six for the navy. Hawley stated that Congress should require that such fields have roughly one thousand acres of flat land, with hangar space to store twenty-four aircraft and buildings to accommodate workshops, machine shops, motor shops, storerooms, officers' quarters and barracks for two hundred enlisted men. Until federally mandated aeronautical stations like Curtiss's Newport News center were established for the military, he iterated, army aviation, in particular, would never amount to much.

The Aero Club of America, Hawley explained, received inquiries every day from people, organizations and newspapers that wanted to know what steps were being taken to immediately equip aviation squadrons with the recommended three aircraft to each aviator. The Aero Club was ashamed to reply that, notwithstanding the lesson of the Europeans embroiled in world war and the United States' Mexican trouble on its southern border, the only action being taken was to order eight aircraft for each squadron. Still, in Newport News, the Aero Club advocated that forty-eight aircraft should be ordered immediately to provide the requisite three aircraft for every army aviator assigned to the Mexican expedition and to organize another aviation corps to hold in reserve in the event of national emergency.

Two days into Hawley and Peary's visit, on April 10, 1916, flight instructor and test pilot Steve MacGordon and Canadian student pilot Walter Drew Hudson set a new American altitude record for an airplane carrying a passenger when MacGordon soared to 14,800 feet in a Curtiss military tractor biplane. MacGordon broke the record previously held by United

As an instructor and test pilot at Curtiss's Newport News Flying School, Victor Carlstrom set world records for speed and distance in the flight of a Curtiss R-7—an R-6 with extended wingspan called *The New York Times*—which he flew on May 20, 1916, from the Atlantic Coast Aeronautical Station to Sheepshead Bay Speedway, New York. He then flew the big 160-horsepower biplane, named for its sponsor and shown here, back to Newport News. Carlstrom covered a distance of 416 miles in four hours, one minute, nonstop, and set the national record at that time for time and distance in continuous flight. *Courtesy of the Library of Congress Prints and Photographs Division.*

States Army Lieutenant Joseph Eugene Carberry at San Diego, California (11,690 feet, set on January 5, 1915). The world record was held by Austrian aviator and Lloyd founder Oberleutnant Heinrich Bier, who flew to an altitude of 20,243 feet on June 27, 1914. MacGordon's flight was his second American record in one month. He was on a hot streak, having set a new cross-country flight record carrying one passenger on April 1, 1916. His trip, from Newport News to Washington, D.C., and back, was a distance of approximately 360 miles, achieved without stopping his engine. Hundreds of people witnessed MacGordon's flight. News that he intended to go after the world altitude record drew widespread attention, and some watchful observers even mistook a flight by Victor Carlstrom as MacGordon going for the record. Carlstrom was just putting a JN-4D through its paces, trying to climb faster and farther with the biplane.

But to further demonstrate the value of aircraft under various weather conditions, MacGordon and Carlstrom had made numerous flights to demonstrate aircraft performance under fifty-seven-mile-per-hour wind for the Aero Club committee. They put the aircraft through every imaginable maneuver, including the loop the loop, which Baldwin normally barred from being performed but permitted for Hawley and the others who observed from the ground below. Also during the club's visit, the station received a new military tractor-type aircraft manufactured by the Sturtevant Aeroplane Company, in business from 1915 to 1918 and formed by its parent company, B.F. Sturtevant Company, to develop military aircraft. The new company was based at Jamaica Plain, Massachusetts. The Sturtevant that arrived in Newport News came with an assembly crew from Curtiss's Buffalo plant and was the first aircraft to have an all-metal fuselage. The company produced a number of these aircraft for both the army and the navy, popularly called the Battle S4 airplane of naval type. The United States Navy bought twelve of the S-design, all metal and highly innovative for aircraft at that period; the army bought four; and the Rhode Island Militia bought one. These seventeen aircraft are recognized as the first all-metal aircraft used by the United States military.

It seemed only fitting that just as the Sturtevant arrived, Curtiss's Newport News flying school took in its first group of military men funded by the Aero Club of America. The officers and enlisted men who arrived in April 1916 were attached to National Guard units from all over the United States and included Captain Ralph L. Taylor, of Connecticut; Lieutenant Bernard Cummings, of Colorado; Lieutenant Edgar Wirt Bagnell, of Nebraska; Lieutenant Howard Franklin Wehrle, of West Virginia, who in 1924 became president of the National Aeronautic Association; Lieutenant Bee Rife Osborne, of Kentucky; Lieutenant Arthur Joseph Coyle, of New Hampshire; Lieutenant Forrest Ward, of Arkansas; Lieutenant Edwin W. Romberger, of Mississippi; and Sergeant Lawton V. Smith, of Georgia.

Another personality who joined this group was civilian Jean Harold Edward Saint Cyr, who married the wealthy widow of James Henry "Silent" Smith, Annie Armstrong Stewart Smith, and was living the high life. He drove a foreign-make touring car that came with a liveried footman and a chauffeur. He told reporters that he was tired of yachting and hoped to find greater pleasure in flying. He'd come to Newport News to find out. But there was something about Saint Cyr that wasn't quite right. A series of articles in the February 1916 *New York World* reported that he was living a dual life, that he was really a missing man named Jack Thompson from Waco, Texas. Thompson was a poor man who'd vanished, only to surface as millionaire

Carlstrom landed on the two-mile oval track at Sheepshead Bay Speedway, built by Blaine Miller and operational from October 9, 1915, to September 20, 1919. There were eight thousand spectators there on May 20, 1916, when Carlstrom touched down in *The New York Times* with his passenger, Connecticut National Guard Captain Ralph L. Taylor, a student

devil-may-care Saint Cyr.

Not all of the daring young men at Newport News were men going off to war. One of them was a young boy, the son of Baldwin's carpenter, Randolph Tucker Wood, who was hired in the fall of 1915 as a mechanic in trade for flying lessons. Charles Terry Wood dropped out of Newport News's John W. Daniel High School to take flight instruction. He soloed in 1916 at the tender age of fifteen, the youngest person to become an aviator in the school's history. Terry Wood didn't stay around the station for very long after he got his certificate. He briefly worked for the National Advisory Committee for Aeronautics (NACA), but that didn't last either. When World War I ended, he took to barnstorming up and down the North Carolina coast with Eddie Stinson's flying circus. He also photographed aerial sequences for the Hollywood movie *Girl from Indiana*. By 1920, Wood had purchased five airplanes and opened his own flying field on Norfolk's old Cottage Toll Road, but this enterprise soon failed due to poor financial planning. Only then did he decide it was probably best to go back to school. At the age of twenty-three, he graduated from Newport News High School. Wood eventually left Hampton Roads for the University of Michigan, where he earned his medical degree. His love of flying, which began at a very young age in a place now gone, never left him and remained a source of joy throughout his life.

Victor Carlstrom flew a 160-horsepower military tractor biplane—a Curtiss R-7, an R-6 with extended wingspan and Curtiss V-X engine sporting the name the *New York Times* for its sponsor—from Newport News on May

pilot at Newport News. Carlstrom's modified R-7 was a one-off aircraft. Taylor, later officer in charge of the army aviation field at Mineola, New York, was killed in an aircraft accident there on August 2, 1917. *Courtesy of the Library of Congress Prints and Photographs Division.*

20, 1916, nonstop to Sheepshead Bay Speedway, a distance of 416 miles, in four hours, one minute. Carlstrom's flight broke the American record for this distance and was officially recorded by the Aero Club of America. But it wasn't without danger. Carlstrom got lost for a short time in a thunderstorm at five thousand feet. Steve MacGordon, who started at the same time from Newport News in another Curtiss plane with student Max Goodnough, was forced to descend to three thousand feet due to the storm's severity. MacGordon didn't reach the speedway until one hour after Carlstrom's arrival. Carlstrom's and MacGordon's flights were executed in connection with a military and civilian aviation tournament held at the Sheepshead Bay Speedway. Carlstrom's passenger was Connecticut national guardsman Captain Ralph L. Taylor, his student. Other pilots who made flights to the speedway from other parts of the country flew off course and, while they eventually arrived safely, set no records. Carlstrom took Aero Club of America President Alan Hawley for a ride high over Sheepshead Bay. Prior to Carlstrom's May 20 flight, the record was 332 miles in four hours, forty-four minutes, made in 1914 between Des Moines, Iowa, and Kentland, Indiana.

Though Vernon Castle had been gone from Newport News for weeks, the May 23, 1916 *Daily Press* reported that Irene Castle returned from England gushing that "Vernon looks 'lovely' in his new Royal Flying Corps uniform. He has already received his wings and expects to go to the front in a week." The Castles danced a command performance before King George V and

National guardsmen from fourteen states became the first noncivilian student pilots at the Atlantic Coast Aeronautical Station when they started flight instruction in April 1916. Standing in front of a Curtiss JN-4D two-seat trainer are (left to right) Second Lieutenant Bernard Cummings, of Colorado; Second Lieutenant Arthur Joseph Coyle, of New Hampshire; Second Lieutenant Edgar Wirt Bagnell, of Nebraska; Dr. Edward George Benson, of Albany, New York; and Second Lieutenant Bee Rife Osborne, of Kentucky. Benson was the "old man" in this picture at age thirty-seven. He died on November 22, 1928, from injuries sustained in an accidental fall. Osborne enlisted in the Kentucky National Guard on September 1, 1915, at age twenty-eight, and made second lieutenant in Company H of the Third Infantry of the Kentucky National Guard on July 6, 1916. He earned his reserve military aviator certification and his FAI pilot license at the Signal Corps Aviation Station, Mineola, New York, that summer. Osborne transferred to active duty with the United States Army Air Service and served during the war in France, where he was eventually promoted to captain. After the war, he returned to Kentucky and became a ticket agent for the Chesapeake and Ohio Railway System. He died on December 22, 1968. Osborne is the first known Kentucky National Guard military aviator. *Courtesy of the George Grantham Bain Collection, Library of Congress Prints and Photographs Division.*

Queen Mary of England at Buckingham Palace while Irene was there to visit Vernon. Two days after Irene's glowing report of Vernon's fortunes, Victor Carlstrom won the twenty-eight-mile airplane race at Sheepshead Bay, New York, taking away the top prize of $500. Carlstrom's time was fourteen minutes, twenty-one seconds; Steve MacGordon came in second with a time of fifteen minutes, thirty-one seconds, winning $300. Female "early bird" Ruth Law finished third in her diminutive Curtiss pusher with a thirty-foot wingspan. Her time was eighteen minutes, sixteen seconds. Law walked away with a $200 purse. MacGordon's victory turned to tragedy when he got back to Newport News.

MacGordon, the pilot who established several American aviation records at Newport News, was severely burned when his Curtiss JN-4D crashed on takeoff on June 5, 1916. He was seated in the front cockpit, normally where his student would have been, and his student took the rear cockpit. Though also burned, his student recovered. MacGordon didn't. He died a painful death two days later. Subsequent investigation revealed that MacGordon's student successfully executed several touch-and-goes and was about to take off again when the engine broke loose from its mount, causing the propeller to strike the ground and drive the engine into the gas tank. Exhaust from the engine set fire to the gasoline, and the aircraft burst into flames. Heat from the fire was so intense that parts of the engine were completely melted. MacGordon's accident was the first serious incident at the station since it opened, and though seven aircraft had been wrecked, none had led to serious injury or death. MacGordon had four students who were expecting to take their final examination with him on June 6, 1916. Carlstrom took his place as their flight instructor.

Baldwin landed in the middle of a heated national argument over the proper training regime for America's national guardsmen in June 1916, right on the heels of MacGordon's death. National guardsmen then being trained at Newport News were soon expected to join the hunt for Pancho Villa on the United States border with Mexico. But lack of available instructor pilots put most of them behind in the training syllabus and jeopardized their future participation to protect America's southern flank for Villa's marauding. Despite concerns expressed by the army and national guard, Baldwin guaranteed that seventeen of his guard student pilots, scheduled to be done by early July, would be ready to go if an army instructor came over to Newport News to supplement Curtiss instructor pilots as earlier promised. His missive didn't help. Newspapers reported that the United States' failure to catch Villa was due to the lack of aircraft and qualified aviators to get the job done. As Baldwin read his June 26, 1916 *Daily Press* morning edition, the words jumped off the page:

> *There is at present no flying corps in the United States service and the National Guardsmen studying here will become the first members of this arm of the service. The United States has few aeroplanes that are little better than junk heaps, and 14 new machines already have been ordered by the government.*

Irene Castle returned from England and reported on May 23, 1916, that "Vernon looks 'lovely' in his new Royal Flying Corps uniform. He has already received his wings and expects to go to the front in a week." While Irene was in England, the couple danced a command performance before the king and queen of England at Buckingham Palace. Vernon is shown here in that Royal Flying Corps uniform and in the company of Jeffrey, his pet monkey. After he was shot down and badly injured, the British flying service sent him to Canada as a flight instructor. After America entered the war, he returned to the United States. The new United States Army Air Service used Vernon as a flight instructor at Benbrook Field, Fort Worth, Texas. *Courtesy of the George Grantham Bain Collection, Library of Congress Prints and Photographs Division.*

Reading down he read an account from the Aero Club of America pertaining to problems faced by American military men fighting in Mexico:

"Most of our difficulties were entirely unexpected," an army flyer reported. "In the rush, our first aim was to get machines where they were so badly needed. Naturally, it was assumed that those aeroplanes which had made records here and there, and those which had given a satisfactory account of themselves abroad, would do the same in Mexico. It was not until we had actual experience on the spot that we discovered new problems due to different conditions. It is a remarkable fact that practically all of the difficulties or other places are mobilized so to speak

Irene Castle posed for this period photograph prior to Vernon's death. Just before Vernon departed for England, the Castles gave two farewell performances at the Hippodrome in New York City with an orchestra conducted by John Philip Sousa. They have been described as the first "pop stars" of the twentieth century, and their fame and fortune certainly attest to it. *Courtesy of the George Grantham Bain Collection, Library of Congress Prints and Photographs Division.*

Irene Castle was off making one of her Astra films on February 15, 1918, when she received word that Vernon had been in a flying accident at an army training field outside Fort Worth, Texas. This time, he didn't walk away. But his student pilot and Jeffrey, his pet monkey, did. Vernon Castle was well liked in the aviation world, so much so that tears streamed down the cheeks of officers and enlisted ground crew who worked to free his mangled body from the wreckage of the plane, shown here. *Courtesy of the George Grantham Bain Collection, Library of Congress Prints and Photographs Division.*

into one united force against us in this part of Mexico. It is that which has made the situation a new problem in aviation. You see, in Mexico we are up against a high temperature, the elevation of Denver, the dry air of Minneapolis, the rising and falling air currents due to the deserts, and soft, light sands covered with low brush. These conditions are the worst possible. On account of the high temperatures, the water in the radiators will reach the temperature of 120 degrees when the motor is not running. This is being overcome by having deeper radiators so as to get more water cooling areas. The sand is so light that the weight of the machine sinks the wheels deeply, making getting away and landing difficult. The sand trouble is being beaten by making new flat tires. Then again at high altitudes, the air is so rarefied that it cuts down the climbing and weight-carrying possibilities of the machines."

Vernon Castle's funeral was held at New York City's Little Church Around the Corner, also called the "Actors' Church." He was buried at Woodlawn Cemetery. Irene Castle is the first woman in the procession following Vernon's casket into the church. *Courtesy of the George Grantham Bain Collection, Library of Congress Prints and Photographs Division.*

The army flyer continued:

> *The chief trouble, however, is with the propellers. Those which stand the tests of several hundred hours' continuous running in the shop, go to pieces in only a few minutes when they are exposed to the Mexican air. The air is so dry that it seems to have an effect on the wood beyond anything we dreamed of. It is so hot down there during the day that the aeroplane mechanics have to cool steel chisels or other metal tools before they can be handled.*

No matter what they read, no matter what they heard, national guardsmen who would soon complete their training at Newport News wanted to join the unnamed army flyer who had just given the world his best description of hell on earth. When graduation day came on July 4, 1916, Fort Monroe's mustering officer came over to claim seventeen guardsmen for army service. But the only man he got was Colorado national guardsman Lieutenant Bernard Cummings. Cummings got a telegram from his state adjutant general asking why he'd mustered in the new United States Army flying corps when he was already a member of the National Guard. Cummings's telegram highlighted the discord between federal and state government over the use of and control over the National Guard. After the Cummings incident, national guardsmen in private aviation schools were sent to New York to complete flight school under the direction of army aviators. Cummings was the first national guardsman to make it through the army's advanced flying corps curriculum.

In the months since it opened, the Atlantic Coast Aeronautical Station had been under the nearly constant observation of men aboard the United States Coast Guard cutter *Onondaga*, berthed close by. Aboard the *Onondaga* were Third Lieutenant Elmer Fowler Stone and Second Lieutenant Norman Hall. Stone would become the coast guard's first aviator and Hall its first aviation engineer, due largely to the enthusiastic support of *Onondaga*'s commanding officer, Captain Benjamin Maurice Chiswell, who invited Glenn Curtiss into his wardroom in 1916 to discuss, with Stone and Hall present, the coast guard's aircraft and pilot training requirement. Soon after, the Virginia Chamber of Commerce petitioned the commonwealth's congressional delegation to support legislation to establish a United States Coast Guard aerial service. Plans for introduction of coast guard aviation were ironed out by Baldwin, who proposed a training syllabus and aircraft acquisition strategy to the coast guard after input from Chiswell, Stone and Hall. Lieutenant Hall was a key participant in Theodore Macaulay's May 4, 1916 record-setting flight in Curtiss's twin-engine H-10 flying boat, the subject of the chapter to follow.

Significant flight test was achieved at the station prior to April 6, 1917, when the United States Navy and Army were committed fully to the war that had waged in Europe for nearly three years. Victor Carlstrom tested an odd plane, a new land and water aircraft unlike anything previously seen at the station. The aircraft mounted a Davis gun, which shot from both the front and rear ends at one time, the rear end belching birdshot and grease, while the front end threw a two-pound shot. The combination flying machine was reputed to be the only one of its kind in the United States. When this aircraft was used on the water, its detachable wheels were removed, and when used on land, the wheels were replaced and adjusted. The change took only moments to complete. This was one of Curtiss's early attempts at an amphibious aircraft. On August 17, 1916, the station debuted the first regulation Curtiss JN-4D Jenny completely built at Newport News. Later in the day, it was taken up for its first flight test and passed.

Newspapers across the country converged on August 19, 1916, to cover

Instructor pilot Steve MacGordon was photographed by Frank Conway at Curtiss's Newport News flight school in early 1916. The numbering of Conway's picture suggests that it was taken sometime between the beginning of January and the end of February that year. Just months later, on June 5, 1916, MacGordon died from injuries sustained in a fiery crash. Captain Baldwin didn't attend MacGordon's funeral. He never attended any of the funerals of those killed at the station. He couldn't bear it. Every man was his responsibility. Of the pilots and students he lost at Newport News, MacGordon's death was arguably the most difficult. *Courtesy of the George Grantham Bain Collection, Library of Congress Prints and Photographs Division.*

what they euphemistically called, for lack of a better title, the William "Bill" Cheyne story. Cheyne was a student at the flying school, but one day he decided to deliver a letter to the midshipman post aboard the battleship USS *Ohio* (BB-12), anchored in Hampton Roads. He didn't want to trust the regular postal service with it, so he penned three epistles in inimitable Harvard flourish, sealed them in an envelope and weighted it down for its trip to the battleship's deck. Cheyne then flew an airplane out over the battleship and dropped the letter on the deck. His fellow students greeted him on the flight line with the lofty title "Father of the United States Airmail Service."

Days later, Lieutenant Albert Paul Schlichting, of the Adams Naval Reserve Unit, flew the *Flying Skillet* with three passengers aboard. The *Flying Skillet* was described as nothing more than a thirty-foot canoe with a motor, wings and propeller—a completely one-off experimental aircraft. But then, on August 21, 1916, Victor Carlstrom took off in the Curtiss Twin

Howard Paul Culver was a student pilot at Newport News in 1916 when Frank Conway took his picture in the cockpit of a Curtiss JN-4D Jenny. Culver's flight instructors were Victor Vernon and Carl Batts. He later soloed in a Curtiss F-boat and received Fédération Aéronautique Internationale Certificate No. 565 on August 25, 1916. Culver also held Aero Club of America Certificate No. 673 and Expert Certificate No. 74. Culver was a test pilot and flight instructor during World War I and an army airmail pilot from May 15 to August 9, 1918. Of the first airmail pilots, Culver was the only one who had more than four months of flying experience. During his airmail service, Culver flew over three thousand miles, logging forty-eight hours of flight time and suffering only one forced landing in thirty-six trips. Culver later founded Culver Engineering Corporation. He died on June 24, 1964, at age seventy-one. *Courtesy of the author.*

JN, a combination landplane/seaplane, for the first of several test flights. The aircraft was capable of coming off the water in twenty seconds from a distance of one thousand feet and could attain a maximum speed of ninety-five miles per hour, thus making it capable of climbing five thousand feet in ten minutes. The Twin JN also sported a state-of-the-art propeller that wasn't yet fitted to any other Curtiss aircraft. "The new machine," Baldwin told reporters, "is as far ahead of anything now in use in the world as sunlight is ahead of starlight. It demonstrated itself the acme of perfection and will minimize danger at least 75 percent." Baldwin further observed that the Twin JN was unquestionably the best all-around aircraft in the world and that the navy's aviation board was "highly pleased" with the success of

Theodore Marsh Hequembourg did not die when he crashed his F-2 flying boat in May 1917, but the accident did inflict serious injuries to him and to naval flying corps student Laurence Curtis. Curtis lost a leg. Hequembourg, shown here prior to that flight, recovered and went to England in October 1918 on military duty. Ted Hequembourg, who earned a bachelor of arts degree from Yale University in 1915, returned there after the war to get a law degree in 1920. Born on May 17, 1894, in Dunkirk, New York, he died in Miami Springs, Florida, on May 21, 1952. Ted's association with the Curtiss Aeroplane and Motor Company began with his older brother, Harry Clarence Hequembourg Jr., who was employed by Glenn Curtiss as a mechanic at his Buffalo, New York manufacturing facility and, later, at Newport News, where the Hequembourg brothers were together just months prior to the accident. *Courtesy of the author.*

Carlstrom's flight test.

There wasn't any reason to doubt Carlstrom's word after he tested an aircraft. He was, after all, the holder of several world records, and within the nation's aviation community, many ranked him the country's top test pilot. During his August 21 flight test of the Twin JN, Carlstrom took several members of the navy's board for a ride, all of them aviators, putting the plane through a battery of flight maneuvers to demonstrate just what it could do. Present that day were three of the navy's most important and first naval aviators: Naval Constructor Commander Holden Chester "Dick" Richardson, Naval Aviator No. 13 and senior officer of the board; Lieutenant Warren Gerald "Gerry" Child, Naval Aviator No. 29; and Lieutenant Clarence King "C.K." Bronson, Naval Aviator No. 15.

Victor Carlstrom set out from Chicago on November 2, 1916, on a nonstop flight to Governors Island, New York, to prove the practicality of cross-continent airplane mail service. Due to mechanical problems with *The New York Times*'s gas feed pipe, Carlstrom was forced down in Erie, Pennsylvania, to make repairs. Despite his layover in Erie, Carlstrom still set a new cross-country nonstop record for the Chicago to Erie leg of the flight and another for the overall time and distance he traveled from Chicago to Governors Island. Carlstrom is pictured describing the flight to Major General Leonard Wood. The photograph was taken shortly after Carlstrom landed on the parade ground at Governors Island on the morning of November 3, 1916. *Courtesy of the Library of Congress Prints and Photographs Division.*

Richardson had already accumulated an impressive record before he set foot at Newport News to observe the Twin JN test. Appointed a naval aviator on April 12, 1915, Richardson served as first secretary of the National Advisory Committee for Aeronautics (NACA) in 1915 and the following year was assigned as construction officer at Naval Air Station Pensacola. By 1918, Richardson had been assigned as the navy's superintendent of aircraft construction at Curtiss's Buffalo manufacturing plant, where he designed the hulls and oversaw the construction and inspection of the Navy/Curtiss, designated NC, flying boats -1 to -4 prior to their May 1919 transatlantic flight. The coast guard's Lieutenant Stone was a member of the crew of the NC-4, which became the first aircraft to successfully fly across the Atlantic. Lieutenant Child was designated a naval aviator on April 29, 1916, and was assigned to Pensacola at the time of his visit to Newport News. Lieutenant Bronson had reported to Pensacola for flight training on May 25, 1914, and had been sent on temporary duty to Curtiss's Buffalo plant on June 6 before assignment that July to the USS *Mississippi* (BB-23), then the navy's aviation training ship. Within a month, Bronson's training was moved over to the USS *North Carolina*, and on October 3, 1914, he was appointed Navy Air Pilot No. 10; this designation was changed to Naval Aviator No. 15 on April 6, 1915. Bronson was killed in the line of duty on November 6, 1916, less than two months after his trip to Virginia to assess the Twin JN.

Three days after Richardson and the others left Newport News, Baldwin announced that Victor Carlstrom would be awarded the 1916 Curtiss Aeroplane and Motor Company trophy and a prize of $7,000 if he could make 700 miles in ten hours flying back and forth between Newport News and Fisherman's Island off Cape Charles, Virginia, with the Curtiss Twin JN. The next day, carrying one passenger, Carlstrom set a new world record when he covered a distance of 641 miles in eight hours, forty minutes. Carlstrom's flight was truncated by carburetor trouble, and two stops to refuel ate up one hour, twenty minutes of his flight time. Despite this, Carlstrom did win the trophy and the money. The Twin JN was in its seaplane configuration when Carlstrom made the flight. Data from the actual flight recorded that Carlstrom burned through 140 gallons of gasoline, which wasn't considered a lot due to the 110 horsepower drawn off each of the aircraft's OXX-2 water-cooled V-8 piston engines.

The Aero Club of America considered Carlstrom's August 1916 flight the most significant aviation achievement of the year. Carlstrom's flying was watched closely by navy and army officers of several countries, as well as foreign manufacturers, all of whom attempted to repeat or best his effort. As a direct consequence of Carlstrom's Twin JN flight, Curtiss's foreign client base ordered more products. "Watch us," said Captain Baldwin to a gathering of newspaper reporters. "We are going after all the world records."

The following day, August 27, four members of the Army Board of Aeronautics came to Newport News to watch Carlstrom fly the Twin JN. Present was Major William Lendrum "Billy" Mitchell. He was on his first trip to Newport News, but it wouldn't be his last. He returned that fall to start flight instruction. He would come down from Washington, D.C., every Friday afternoon on an Old Bay Line steamer, take lessons all day Saturday and Sunday and then sail back home on Sunday night. His instructor was Jimmy Johnson. But Walter Lees also took part in Mitchell's training, supervising its final stage. In a letter located in the National Air and Space Museum archive, Walter Lees wrote:

> *Jimmy Johnson should have the credit of really teaching him* [Mitchell]
> *to fly. Jim took sick one week end* [sic] *and Captain Baldwin turned Billy*

Ruth Law flew an old Curtiss pusher from Chicago to Governors Island, New York, on November 19–20, 1916, to better Victor Carlstrom's earlier feat. While her elapsed time was slower than that made by Carlstrom two weeks earlier, she covered 884 miles in eight hours, fifty-five minutes and thirty-five seconds. She flew 590 miles of it without putting down, which was the longest nonstop flight in American history up to that time. Law had never before flown a cross-country flight. She is shown here with Major General Leonard Wood, who came out to greet her when she landed. The next day, she flew into New York City with United States Army Lieutenant Henry Harley "Hap" Arnold as her passenger. President Woodrow Wilson attended a dinner in her honor on December 2, 1916. *Courtesy of the George Grantham Bain Collection, Library of Congress Prints and Photographs Division.*

over to me, and after several hours' instruction he was hot, and I turned him loose. He took more instruction after that, and we all know what a fine pilot he turned out to be.

Mitchell had his first flight lesson on September 4, 1916. Curtiss might disagree somewhat with Lees's assessment of Mitchell's flying. At the end of his first solo flight, Major Mitchell crashed his Curtiss JN-4D Jenny. The aircraft was a total loss. Mitchell wasn't hurt, but he was left hanging upside down strapped in the cockpit. After being cut out of the harness, his widely reported first words were purportedly, "Now, what did I do wrong?"

Early that September, the United States government placed an order for fifty Curtiss Twin JN aircraft. They carried a price tag of $14,000 each. The army had also announced that Newport News would become the primary training ground for United States Army pilots. Optimistically, Baldwin hedged that before the year was over, one thousand aviators would be trained in the waning months of 1916 under the army air service's reorganization plan. The only army aviation school up to that time was located in San Diego, California.

Billy Mitchell returned to Newport News with three other army officers to observe the Dep flight control system. The army entrusted Mitchell with organization of its air service, which at the time included establishing a flight school system and training program. The day after Mitchell had taken his first lesson, Baldwin prematurely told the press that the school's current effort would redouble in the coming months to accommodate an expected influx of army officers in flight training. Someday, he told them, the aeronautical station would become to the airplane world what Detroit was to the automobile world. He expected the first group of new army aviation candidates to start arriving on September 15; most of them were recent college graduates. The curriculum that he and Mitchell drew up included rigid physical and mental examination before the start of coursework. This differed from the process previously used to evaluate civilians who had already gone through the station's flight instruction program. Flying lessons were no longer offered to men and women who were ineligible to join a military flying corps. Now, all who stepped onto the flight line at Newport News were bound for military aviation.

A group of fresh army aviation students had just arrived when, on October 7, 1916, flight instructor Victor Vernon and mechanic Percy Platt Kirkham crashed a Twin JN into Hampton Roads with so much force of impact that it smashed the pontoons and the plane turned turtle in the water. This was something a new class of trainees didn't need to see so soon after their arrival. Vernon and Kirkham weren't hurt, but the Twin JN was a total loss.

After the army decided to relocate the lion's share of its flight training to Newport News, the story that ran in the October 18, 1916 *Daily Press* shocked everyone. The headline suggested that the city would lose the aeronautical station and its military training program.

> *The city may lose the aviation plant at the boat harbor. Unless the government plant is established here, the Atlantic Coast Aeronautical Station will amount to little. Neither the city, nor any civic or commercial organization has moved so much as a finger in aiding in the attempt to bring the government station here. Report has it that most people having land suitable for the government aviation field are holding it at exorbitant prices. The location of the government station would be one of the biggest things in the history of the city, while if it goes to Florida, this city will become practically dead in aviation circles. Unless the government plant is located here, Captain Baldwin will go to Florida.*

The following day, the *Daily Press* followed up with a story that reported:

> *The municipal industrial commission and the* [Newport News] *Chamber of Commerce has advised Captain Baldwin that they are ready to do all they can to secure additional landing ground for the proposed government aviation school.*

The property owner, the widow of H.B. Hoover, held on to ninety acres in the middle of a four-hundred-acre tract the army acquired for Langley Field. The ongoing dust-up over the Hoover property plagued Langley's development for months. Curtiss and Baldwin had already considered the same land for an expanded aeronautical station. But they had not acted on it. Hoover wanted too much money for the parcel.

Baldwin's October 26 response assured local government that the Atlantic Coast Aeronautical Station would remain at the municipal small boat harbor, and the following day he once again prematurely and errantly announced the acquisition of three hundred acres to the station's property with a clear-cut plan to build additional hangar space. His specificity seemed to assuage the chamber and industrial commission. But the three hundred acres didn't exist, and neither did any plan to add to buildings not already standing on the property. Baldwin told them what they wanted to hear, not what was going to happen.

Back at the station, word came that Buck Gallop, accompanied by several men who had graduated from Curtiss's Newport News flying school just after him, had left Washington, D.C., on November 1 to take his army

The men didn't get all the glory. Mary Anita "Neta" Snook arrived at Newport News, having left Iowa State College, to take flight lessons on July 21, 1916, at Newport News, Virginia. She later recalled, "When not in class [at Iowa State] I spent much of my time at the college library. There, I read all about balloons and learned of the daring feats of young Tom Baldwin…I also read about heavier-than-air craft—planes that used mechanical power. Now I really wanted to learn to fly." But she didn't find her idol so receptive. Baldwin said no. A woman killed in an aircraft crash might brand aviation unsafe. She went back to Iowa and tried again, returning on October 5, 1916. This time, Eddie Stinson took her flying and showed her some aerobatics, and Stewart Wellesley "Andrew" Cogswell came to the rescue and told Baldwin he would teach her to fly. She finished training and was about to solo when the United States declared war on Germany on April 6, 1917. Civilian flight training ended. She is shown here standing on the wing of a Curtiss JN-4D. Cogswell is in the rear cockpit. The year was 1917, and the photographer was Frank Conway. *Courtesy of the author.*

aviation service entrance exam. This was welcome news. The next day, a Chinese aviation candidate arrived from Honolulu to start flight instruction. Sen Yet Yong was wealthy but ambitious. He made the papers on November 24, after he invited Baldwin, Walter Lees, Jack Colgan and his entire flight school class to a chop suey dinner at the Chinese Café in Norfolk. After the ceremonial round of tea, bird nest soup was served, followed by shark fin. Almond chicken was next, followed by fried spring chicken. Edward Antoine "Buffalo" Bellande was nearly kept from eating anything at all when his chopsticks wouldn't behave. After some debate among the pilots, Bellande was finally allowed to eat with a fork. He was only eighteen years old and the youngest member to graduate from a Newport News class in December

1916. Over dinner, Yong explained to everyone that his purpose in coming to Newport News for flight instruction was to learn to fly for himself, yes, but more importantly, he wanted to bring aviation home to the Hawaiian people. Yong was not the only foreign celebrity at Newport News at that time. Karl von Wrede, of Finnish nobility, arrived that November, too.

The same day Yong arrived at Newport News, on November 2, 1916, Victor Carlstrom started his nonstop flight from Chicago, Illinois, to Governors Island, New York, to prove the practicality of cross-continent airplane mail service. On board his modified two-hundred-horsepower Curtiss JN-4D Jenny, named *The New York Times* for its sponsor, he carried over one thousand letters and postcards addressed to people around the country, including President Woodrow Wilson, Colonel Theodore Roosevelt, Major General Leonard Wood, Thomas Edison and many others. The flight didn't go off as planned. *The New York Times*'s gas feed pipe broke, forcing Carlstrom to put down at Erie, Pennsylvania, for repairs. Though he wasn't able to make it to Governors Island nonstop, Carlstrom still set a new cross-country record. His 452-mile nonstop flight from Chicago to Erie was achieved in four hours, seventeen minutes and thirty seconds. From Erie, he flew to Hammondsport, New York, for the night and continued on to Governors Island the next morning, landing on the parade ground at 8:55 a.m. in the presence of Major General Leonard Wood, commanding officer of the United States Army's Department of the East. The total distance flown by Carlstrom was 967 miles, and his flight time was eight hours, twenty-eight minutes and thirty seconds, with an average speed of 114 miles per hour. Many months later, the first official airmail flight, flown between New York City and Washington, D.C., was achieved on May 15, 1918. A simultaneous flight from Washington, D.C., to New York City failed when its army pilot flew in the wrong direction and landed in a farmer's field south of the nation's capital.

Certainly, the women who took rides with Curtiss's instructor pilots had their own stories to tell. Lucy Fields, whose glorious mezzo-soprano voice dazzled audiences from London to New York, showed up at the field on December 5 to get a ride with Ted Hequembourg in a Curtiss flying boat. The flight didn't start out well, and it definitely didn't end that way. Before she climbed into the right seat, Fields made a mechanic wipe it off because it was wet and she didn't want to ruin her skirt. As he took off, salt spray came up in her face. But that wasn't the worst of it. Hequembourg was starting back to the seaplane dock after spiraling down from one thousand feet, and nothing seemed wrong. But as he tried to straighten the plane for landing about one hundred feet over the water, his controls failed. The aircraft came down in the water at the end of the Ivy Avenue pier. Fields

Of the dozen or so photographs in my collection of Neta Snook at Newport News taken over the course of her training there, those that follow are favorites. She is shown here standing in front of a Curtiss JN-4D. Snook was as skilled at working on aircraft as she was flying them. To pay for flying lessons, she went to work in Baldwin's machine shop overhauling OX-5 engines. When she left Hampton Roads in 1917, Snook became an expeditor for the British War Mission in Canada, inspecting the assembly of Curtiss OX-5 engines. When the war ended on November 11, 1918, she bought a wrecked Canuck, the Canadian version of a Curtiss JN-4D Jenny, rebuilt it and, in the spring of 1920, trailered the plane to a level pasture and flew it solo, thus completing what she'd been denied three years earlier at Newport News. *Courtesy of the author.*

Neta Snook, photographed by Frank Conway at Newport News in 1917, often mugged for the camera, and he clearly enjoyed it. She's doing that here. Snook moved to Los Angeles in the fall of 1920 and opened her own flight school at W.B. "Bert" Kinner's new airfield in the South Gate area of the city. She was already a nationally known exhibition pilot, and it didn't take long for Kinner to make her the test pilot for his new aircraft, the Kinner Airster. She later wrote on the back of a photograph of herself with the Airster that "I test flew it and Amelia bought it." During one of her Airster exhibitions in December 1920, she met Amelia Earhart. She taught Amelia to fly. Without Neta Snook, there would have been no legendary Amelia Earhart. *Courtesy of the author.*

and Hequembourg weren't seriously hurt, but the flying boat was completely wrecked. He remembered later that she got a little wet and was awfully mad. The skirt she'd tried so hard not to ruin was destroyed when the cockpit filled with water and she had to swim for it. The star of Victor Herbert's *Gypsy Love* wasn't in love with a flying boat.

The first anniversary of the Atlantic Coast Aeronautical Station, December 10, 1916, came with a public warning from Captain Baldwin. Despite the local population's familiarity with seeing aircraft in the sky overhead, they didn't know how to move around them on the ground. Baldwin's admonishment was directed to the parents of children who were permitted to play on or near the station. There had been a significant number of serious, and almost fatal, accidents in which a child walked into or too close to a spinning propeller. Others had come close to being struck by landplanes taking off and landing. Aircraft accidents, whether in the air or on the ground, were costly to the industry. Curtiss knew this was true, and he'd always worried that pilot and passenger deaths would have a negative impact on future aircraft research and development. The public would shy away from what it feared. He didn't want them to fear airplanes. MacGordon's death had a ripple effect, and predictably, the public believed what he was doing when he died was unsafe. But the worst hadn't happened yet.

Victor Carlstrom, arguably America's top test pilot, took off with student Cary B. Epes on May 9, 1917. The flight was routine. Carlstrom wasn't trying to put the Curtiss JN-4D through aerobatic maneuvers. There wasn't any fancy flying involved. This was Epes's first flight. Carlstrom's younger brother, Carl, who had just completed flight training himself, was standing below, watching the flight. Then it happened. At thirty-five hundred feet, Carlstrom leveled off the aircraft, and the right wing peeled back. There was nothing he could do. The wing crumpled, flapping like tissue paper as the biplane spiraled to the ground. Carl Carlstrom saw it all. Walter Lees had just come out of the hangar when he heard the unmistakable sound of Carlstrom's Jenny diving nose first into the field. "I rushed to the plane to pull them out," he told a reporter.

> *There was no fire, but the nose of the plane was buried three feet into the ground. Both of them were cut pretty bad, and blood was everywhere. Neither of them moved, but I couldn't tell whether they were dead or just knocked out. When we got them out, we knew they were dead. It was a shock. Vic had been one of my closest friends. We had been laughing and joking just before he went up.*

The Jenny's wing had recently been broken and repaired. In the face of the accusation that the aircraft should never have been flown again, Baldwin denied that it was defective. Clearly, it was. Baldwin repeated that each aircraft was thoroughly checked for structural and mechanical problems prior to every flight. But no one would ever know the truth. Carlstrom's and Epes's lips were sealed in death, and witnesses all saw something different before the aircraft struck the ground. Consensus was reached about the right wing: it separated from the aircraft before impact. Authorities had, without question, hundreds of witnesses to the death spiral that took the lives of Carlstrom and his student. Some turned their backs at the last moment so they wouldn't have to remember the look of horror on the faces of the men trapped inside. Some covered their ears so they wouldn't hear the screams. Pilots didn't wear parachutes at the time. By day's end, most of Curtiss's instructors and students had visited the wreckage, devastated by the loss. Among Carlstrom's observant colleagues was instructor pilot Lawrence Leon, who emigrated from Italy in 1913 and three years later earned his Fédération Aéronautique Internationale pilot license at Curtiss's Buffalo flying school. He was an instructor at the Atlantic Coast Aeronautical Station from January through August 1917.

The Carlstrom-Epes tragedy was compounded by "what could have been." Newport News native Epes was engaged to be married to Margaret Temple of Danville, Virginia. Carlstrom was moving on, too. He was engaged to Sallie Blassingham, also of Newport News, and he'd just been commissioned a first lieutenant in the army officers' reserve corps but hadn't yet been called to active duty. He was more valuable to the army at the time teaching at the aeronautical station. His and Cary Epes's deaths were the fourth and fifth fatalities since the school opened. This wasn't altogether a bad record. "Flying is a dangerous, chancy business," said Baldwin. "Aviators are going to be killed from time to time. Carlstrom's death is a terrible loss to the school, but we've got to continue. The future of aviation is still ahead of us." Six days later, Ted Hequembourg and naval aviation student Laurence Curtis crashed in a flying boat from an altitude of seventy-five feet. Curtis lost a leg. Hequembourg broke his back but recovered.

After the Hequembourg-Curtis accident, the military pilot pool at Newport News grew beyond what Baldwin anticipated. When the weather at Buffalo deteriorated to the point of interfering with flight instruction, Curtiss sent the entire class down to Virginia. He did this several times over the winter and early spring. One of the men he transferred to Newport News was Rochester, New York native Donald Barnum "Doc" Alvord, born February 27, 1892. Alvord graduated in 1915 from Columbia University as an architecture major. He didn't get to Newport News until after Victor Carlstrom's death. Alvord roomed with instructor pilot Eddie Stinson and would later recall that he and Stinson "flipped a coin to see who would sleep in the bed of a *New York Times* reporter who had been killed in a flying accident the day before we arrived. I lost. I'm not really superstitious," Alvord opined, "but I didn't sleep too well that Saturday night." Despite the station's rash of misfortune, the navy also contracted the Curtiss Aeroplane and Motor Company to train twenty men of its Naval Reserve Flying Corps (NRFC) at Newport News. This was fine with Doc Alvord. He was already living in cramped quarters. The more the merrier. Alvord's instructor was Carl Carlstrom. Records also show that he was taught by Stewart Cogswell.

Doc Alvord had arrived at Newport News as a civilian, but on July 28, 1917, as was customary in the naval service, he first enlisted as a seaman second class at a predetermined location, in his case Washington, D.C., with instructions

Taken at Newport News during her instruction with Stewart Cogswell, Neta Snook is propping the Curtiss JN-4D Jenny to get it started. Despite her unique status as the first and most significant woman to take flight training through Curtiss's Atlantic Coast Aeronautical Station, Snook remained humble. But she was a natural, intuitive pilot. Captain Baldwin recognized her skill and respected her. She is included in all group shots taken by Frank Conway at the field while she was a resident student. In the decade that followed World War I, she flew exhibitions and was a crowd pleaser. *Courtesy of the author.*

Though she will always be remembered for teaching Amelia Earhart to fly, Neta Snook was the first female aviator in Iowa, the first female student accepted at the Curtiss Flying School in Newport News, Virginia, the first woman to run her own flying business and the first woman to run a commercial airfield in the United States. She was, in truth, one of the first female aviators in the country. Born in Salem, Mount Carroll, Illinois, on February 14, 1896, Neta Snook Southern died in Santa Clara, California, on March 23, 1991, at age ninety-five. She struck this pose in the cockpit of her Curtiss JN-4D Jenny at Newport News in 1917. *Courtesy of the author.*

to return to the Atlantic Coast Aeronautical Station as a Naval Reserve Flying Corps officer candidate to complete flight training before reporting to ground school at the Massachusetts Institute of Technology (MIT). After successful completion of his coursework at MIT, Alvord was sent to Pensacola, Florida. But before any of that happened, Alvord had to get through Newport News. During the fall of 1917, he came close to destroying a trolley car packed with men, women and children when he flew too low over Jefferson Avenue in a Curtiss Jenny. He pulled up just in time but crash-landed across the street, coming to rest in a diner. No one was hurt badly, but the biplane's propeller was wedged in the lunch counter. He'd had a close call.

After Carlstrom's death, flight test continued. Eddie Stinson took his place. Stinson flew *The Duck*, Alvord later recalled. He flew it because no one else would go near it.

> *One day Stinson said, "I just gotta fly that damned duck, and I'm sure it will be the death of me." We got up early one morning, and I went out to the end of the runway to make sure Eddie would safely clear the*

trees, which bordered the edge of the field. Ed's engine conked out as he was over the hedgerow, and he turned back, just making the runway. The wheels of The Duck went off the side into some swampy ground, turning the tail straight up in an abrupt stop. I ran over and undid his seat belt. Ed was a bit shaken up, though glad that The Duck was now permanently out of commission.

On the way back to the hangar, Stinson told Alvord, "I've got to fly right now again before I quit today." They wheeled out a Jenny for him to take up. "Then and there," Alvord continued,

he broke the world looping record with 102 consecutive loops. The next day he said to me, "You and I are going to do the first two-passenger loop without power that has ever been made." And, so far as I know, we did it. I was scared to death, of course—then, and many times afterward.

Several world records for speed and stunt flying were set by Eddie Stinson, later manufacturer of the Stinson plane, at Newport News. He set a record by performing two loop the loop maneuvers in rapid succession in a two-ton flying boat while carrying a passenger, Doc Alvord, on August 3, 1917, before training regulations forbade them. The feat, considered impossible before Stinson did it, prompted Baldwin to say that it was the most remarkable thing he'd ever witnessed. Stinson skillfully put the aircraft into a twenty-five-degree bank, applied reverse rudder and held the flying boat without losing balance. The Curtiss R-6 that Stinson used for the stunt had a wingspan of nearly seventy feet and a 250-horsepower engine. Two days later, on August 5, Stinson looped eleven times, swooping down to within fifty feet of Newport News rooftops as thousands of people watched his remarkable flying exhibition. On August 7, Stinson broke all American records by looping twenty-two times in rapid succession. The *Daily Press* reported that Stinson's aerial antics had become a daily feature. The month of August 1917 belonged to Eddie Stinson. But on August 10, Butch Hautz thought he'd get in on Stinson's action and pulled off five consecutive loop the loops. He described the experience as "standing on your head in the air."

Alvord graduated flight training at Newport News on December 6, 1917. He was commissioned an ensign in the Naval Reserve Flying Corps and winged at Pensacola on January 8, 1918. He was designated Naval Aviator No. 225. Alvord remained at Pensacola flying the Curtiss Jenny and R-6. He didn't make it to England until after the war. He did some postwar patrol flying from Yarmouth, Felixstowe, Lough Foyle, Queenstown and Bolsena before coming home.

The war that took so many lives "over there" also claimed one important life at home. Vernon Castle had been gone from Newport News for nearly two years, but his popularity in and out of uniform never waned. He had flown dangerous reconnaissance missions over Germany, taking surveillance photographs for which an appreciative French government awarded him the Croix de Guerre. But Castle was shot down and so badly injured that the British sent him to Canada to work as a flight instructor. Castle was an excellent teacher. After the United States entered the war, the new United States Army Air Service used him as a flight instructor at Benbrook Field, Fort Worth. While students of this period routinely sat in the front cockpit during training, Castle changed up the seating arrangement after a crash in which he walked away but the student in the front seat died. From that point forward, he insisted on taking the front cockpit.

On February 15, 1918, Castle motioned for his student to take the backseat. Irene was making one of her Astra films, believed to have been *The Mysterious Client*, when she got word that Vernon was in another accident. This time, she was told, he didn't make it. But his student did, and he would have wanted it to be that way. Vernon Castle's funeral was held at New York City's Little Church Around the Corner, also called the "Actors' Church." He was buried at prestigious Woodlawn Cemetery. Irene was so grieved by his death that she posed for a nude, life-size bronze statue of her willowy form bent over in deep mourning. The statue was placed over Vernon's grave. Though she would marry three more times, when she died on January 25, 1969, Irene was buried with Vernon, her first and only true love. An impressive monument was later erected at the site of Castle's crash in Benbrook, Texas. It reads: "Neither the other pilot, his student cadet, nor Vernon's pet monkey, Jeffrey, were seriously injured." On the other side of the monument is a graceful, windy poem written by Ruth Finley in 1918 that appropriately captured Castle's life: "He danced and gave his dearest gift; That little children yet unborn; May dance with gay, unshackled feet; To tunes not piped by Battle's horn."

3
SOARING THROUGH THE AIR

The Atlantic Coast Aeronautical Station had only been open a few days when aviation instructor and test pilot Theodore Charles Macaulay arrived at Newport News. Macaulay's association with Curtiss went back to 1912. Curtiss sent him through his San Diego flight school, and Macaulay came out in May 1913 with his Fédération Aéronautique Internationale pilot license and a job as chief instructor and manager of Curtiss's San Diego and Toronto flight schools. He took part in extensive flight tests of Curtiss flying boats, which landed him in Newport News in 1916. Macaulay left Curtiss in the spring of 1916 to pursue a contract in Imperial Russia and, after that, to become one of the first civilian instructors at the newly established United States Army Signal Corps Aviation School in Chicago, Illinois. When the United States got into the war, he transferred with the signal corps to Rockwell Field, San Diego, and was commissioned a first lieutenant. He advanced rapidly to major, and during World War II, he was promoted to colonel and worked with the army air corps. He had an incredible career. But the "incredible" in his career began with the worldwide recognition he received for his record-breaking flights from Newport News in May 1916.

On May 4, 1916, Ted Macaulay lifted a Curtiss H-10 hydroaeroplane off the waters of Hampton Roads and declared the flight "up" at 1:35 p.m. Fitted with two 160-horsepower motors, this was Curtiss's newest flying boat. With this aircraft, Macaulay established eleven new world records and one new American altitude record for a plane carrying a pilot and five passengers. Macaulay's flight was the greatest event to happen to the Curtiss station in its history and came on the heels of the last great period of Curtiss's Newport News experimental

Glenn Curtiss's Newport News flying school and aircraft test facility was a major public draw for its weekend flight exhibition and aircraft display. Frank Conway photographed the crowd that had gathered along the water's edge and around the main hangar of the aeronautical station in 1916. *Courtesy of the author.*

station before America's involvement in World War I. Macaulay would set new marks for duration; distance, closed circuit; distance, straight line; speeds from ten to two hundred kilometers; and for greatest speed per hour flight of five kilometers. Until his 1916 flights, most of the world records he would break were held by France's Roland Garros.

Macaulay's flight plan included making Baltimore, Maryland, nonstop. But the H-10 hit a severe thunderstorm off Point Lookout, 85 miles from Newport News on the Chesapeake Bay. When he put down, Macaulay had covered 164 miles in two hours, twenty-three minutes. He was accompanied on the flight by Alessandro Pomilio, of the Italian Royal Flying Corps; Second Lieutenant Norman Hall, of the United States Coast Guard; Chief Mechanic Phillip Utter, of the Curtiss Aeroplane and Motor Company; and Charley Good, a student. There was also an unnamed Norfolk newspaper reporter on board. During the flight, Hall conducted tests on a new drift compass as a navigational aid aboard a military aircraft. Using the compass, Hall was able to aid course accuracy from Newport News up the Chesapeake Bay and back to Newport News. An improved version of Hall's drift compass was used three years later on the NC-4 transatlantic flight.

In addition to teaching high-profile students like United States Army Major Billy Mitchell on weekends, Thomas Baldwin's flight instructors doubled as exhibition and test pilots. They were crowd pleasers. Men, women and children who flocked to the Atlantic Coast Aeronautical Station to watch them fly were not just from Hampton Roads. Spectators also came from up and down the East Coast to check out Curtiss's "southern experiment." Frank Conway took this picture in 1916 of a Curtiss JN-4D Jenny taking off at Newport News. *Courtesy of the author.*

The May 4 flight was just the beginning. The trip lived up to Baldwin's billing. He told the crew before they pushed off from the pier, "Remember, there's nothing like your first trip. You're in for a great experience this time. Your later trips will be commonplace, but this one I envy you." Utter cranked one of the engines to get it started and then the other. The reporter on board journaled that as the boat gathered speed, a little spray came over the bow.

> *The motors picked up until the propellers just behind your head were roaring. The body of the boat seemed to lift a bit in the water. You saw the faces of the others relax slightly. You wondered why and then it occurred to you that the H-10 had begun to plane.*

Within moments, the H-10 was making about forty miles an hour; at least, that's what it felt like. "By the time you looked over the side to verify this," the reporter opined, "you found the wind was rushing past your face with such force you could, with difficulty, keep your eyes above the cockpit edge. You felt the big hull lifting in the water. The prow [nose] began to lift sharply upward." Soon enough, the H-10 crew felt the unmistakable sensation of the aircraft skipping off the water. Each skip was a little longer than the one before it, five or six in all. "And suddenly," he wrote, "the boat seemed

Curtiss had a seaplane ramp built over the beach to the water, and it was from this location that onlookers came on weekends and sometimes during the week to watch the air show. Two Curtiss F-boats, one on the ramp and one in the air overhead, are shown in this 1916 picture. The Curtiss Model F was a pusher flying boat that carried a crew of two. Curtiss used the aircraft as a primary trainer at Newport News. The instructor and student sat side by side in a single cockpit forward of the wings and below the motor. The wing configuration of these aircraft changed through 1918. While some of them had wings of equal span, others had an overhanging top wing to increase lift. There are many other differences that identify early versus late models of this aircraft. The F-boat was powered by a single one-hundred-horsepower Curtiss OXX engine. *Courtesy of the Sargeant Memorial Room, Norfolk Public Library.*

unusually steady. She had stopped 'skipping.' You didn't feel the pressure of the water against the hull. You peeped over the side to look at the water and you could see no water." The H-10 was airborne.

> *Cautiously, because you didn't know whether the movement of your body would affect the balance of the craft, you craned your neck over the side and looked down. The surface of Hampton Roads had dropped away from you. You were going at terrific speed and rising rapidly through the air. And then, while you were still almost breathless with trying to keep track of the new sensations that were crowding upon you, the H-10 reached an altitude of about 900 feet and began to swing in a long curve around the Roads and towards Old Point Comfort. You caught your first, long, stock-taking breath and with it the exhilaration that flying brings.*

Soaring Through the Air

This is a wide view of a 1916 crowd gathered at the Atlantic Coast Aeronautical Station to watch an F-boat demonstration. *Courtesy of the Sargeant Memorial Room, Norfolk Public Library.*

Over the heads of the aircraft's crew, the motors hummed their rhythmic plaint. Peering forward, crewmen felt the rush of the wind pressing their goggles against their faces as the flying boat cut through the air at ninety miles per hour. Behind the reporter sat Macaulay. He had turned from the smiling young man who'd greeted his crew at the station the night before into a serious aviator. One of his crew noticed that Macaulay had a crease in his forehead. "He looked straight ahead, almost fixedly. His lips were parted and he moistened them constantly with his tongue. It seemed he was listening intently for something." Utter, a flight mechanic, listened too. While Macaulay stared straight ahead, Utter eyed the engines critically, listening to their roar for sounds of trouble.

Taken in by the experience, the reporter, who had never before flown in an airplane of any kind, wrote:

> *By this time the exhilaration of the thing had gotten into your blood. You felt, with senses unusually acute, the drive of the big boat, soaring through the air on even keel more steadily and with less vibration than any fast train, speed boat or automobile you had ever ridden in; the rush of the wind on your temples; the dominating song of the motors. Nearly*

Major Billy Mitchell brought his family on a number of visits to Curtiss's Newport News airfield in the spring and summer of 1916. Captain Thomas Baldwin is shown here with Mitchell's daughters, Harriet (left) and Elizabeth (right), and Mitchell's first wife, the former Caroline Stoddard of Rochester, New York. The couple had three children, including a son, John Lendrum III, born on January 20, 1920. The Mitchells divorced in 1922. *Courtesy of the author.*

> *a thousand feet below swiftly unfolded the changing panorama of water and land.*

As Macaulay turned the H-10 over the curvature of Old Point Comfort there were three battleships anchored in Hampton Roads. "The battleships brought to your mind [Rudyard] Kipling's line, 'Sky-hooting through the brine.' You thought 'sky-hooting' was exactly what the H-10 was doing." The H-10 cleared the point, the Chamberlin Hotel on the right. It quickly cleared Fort Wool and Fort Monroe with their gun positions exposed and dwarfed looking down from high in the air. At Thimble Shoals Light, Macaulay changed course for the Back River. As the H-10 answered its rudder, Macaulay's passengers got their first glimpse of the Virginia Capes and all the ships coming and going far below. Ribbons of smoke trailed behind tiny steamers, and a small fleet of schooners moved along under sail. A wake of foam and divided water stretched far astern of each vessel. The H-10 followed the ship channel up the Chesapeake Bay. Past the Back River and over York Spit, the log of the H-10 noted the aircraft

An instructor pilot and student stood off to the right on the seaplane ramp to let mechanics complete a preflight inspection of a Curtiss F-boat. The aircraft had been wheeled out of its hangar and down the ramp on a cradle pulled by a horse. With the aircraft in place at the end of the ramp, it was up to mechanics, ground crew and the tide to get the aircraft in and out of Hampton Roads. The man dressed in waders to the far right and holding the port wing strut played an important part in the next two photographs of this rare 1916 F-boat launch and recovery sequence at Newport News. *Courtesy of the Sargeant Memorial Room, Norfolk Public Library.*

covered six miles in four minutes doing ninety miles per hour. Half an hour of "sky-hooting" was freedom. "You were flying. Nothing else mattered."

There were clouds floating just above the flying boat, their shadows moving across the bay, dark patches on ruffled velvet. When the sun came out through the clouds, its rays fell on the wings of the H-10 with an effect like that when sunlight strikes the wings of a gull wheeling over the sea. Charley Good tapped on his friends in the aft cockpit and pointed out two Chesapeake Bay bugeyes racing, their canvasses drawing and white sails swelled out in the breeze. The boats were observed to be evenly matched. The shadow of the H-10 cast the shadow of an enormous sea bird, its poised wings, head and tail all sharply defined on the sea below.

Over the Rappahannock River, the river was a silver thread stretching its way to the northwest with its sinuous curves, its peninsulas and estuaries etched as delicately as a fine steel engraving. It wasn't until he'd reached the Rappahannock that Macaulay ran into severe turbulence. As he neared the

The Curtiss F-boat shown in the prior photograph was given a final push in the water by the ground crewman wearing waders. *Courtesy of the Sargeant Memorial Room, Norfolk Public Library.*

Potomac's north bank, the sun was nearly entirely obscured by clouds and the air was noticeably cooler.

Off Point Lookout, eighty-two miles from Newport News, the wind blew for a short time with gale force. Out of the northwest came a sharp squall with a few premonitory raindrops, which came down horizontally and struck the crew sharply in the face. The sudden gust of wind that followed felt like an Arctic blast. Then came a short lull followed by spitting rain that battered them all with the force of needle pricks poking skin. When some of Macaulay's crew reached up to cover their eyes with goggles, they were surprised to find them gone. The rain and wind had carried them away. Macaulay flew without his. Those who could ducked below the H-10's deck level to escape the rain that now pounded them steadily. Macaulay couldn't retreat. He pressed on until he couldn't go farther. He turned the H-10 back the way he'd come and headed south.

Within moments of turning around, the H-10 broke into sunlit sky, winging its way back to Newport News. Ten minutes later, out of the corner of his eye, Macaulay caught Utter digging around in his toolbox. But by then he'd heard what Utter saw. Even an untrained ear could have heard the variation in the sound of the H-10's slowing engine. A liquid stream about the size of

When the Curtiss F-boat later returned to the Atlantic Coast Aeronautical Station, the tide was up, making it easier for the man in waders to guide it back up the ramp and onto its cradle. *Courtesy of the Sargeant Memorial Room, Norfolk Public Library.*

Frank Conway was sitting in the right seat of a Curtiss F-boat when he took this photograph of the Atlantic Coast Aeronautical Station (right) in the spring of 1916. *Courtesy of the author.*

By the middle of March 1916, the newspapers had gotten wind that the Atlantic Coast Aeronautical Station had "a giant flying boat of the American-type [that] is rapidly being put together," but it was not to be used until the hangar being built especially for the boat was finished. Articles described the flying boat as a twin-engine, 320-horsepower aircraft capable of carrying four or five men, "one of the largest of its kind in existence." Workers are shown in this photograph, and in the one to follow, enlarging the main hangar to accommodate assembly of the Curtiss H-10 flying boat. *Courtesy of the author.*

a man's little finger poured from the fuel feed pipe at the carburetor intake. The disabled engine wasn't going to be an easy to fix. Located between the upper and lower wings, several feet out from aircraft fuselage, it couldn't be reached from the cockpit. Utter couldn't let the H-10 continue to bleed fuel either. He had to climb out between the wings to make the repair.

Utter fished out a roll of adhesive tape, put it between his teeth and clambered out of the cockpit. As he edged himself onto the wing, the wind whipped his overalls so hard they were torn to tatters. Ignoring this, he braced himself against the wing supports, caught the piano wire stay and wriggled out from there to reach the H-10's crippled motor. There was nothing between him and the Chesapeake Bay but a thin wing and a thousand feet of sky. As he braced himself with his feet, Utter took the tape from his mouth, reached up with both hands to wind the feed pipe and waited to see the result of his handiwork. He was successful. Slowly, he made his way back to the cockpit, and the motor gradually picked up

The two women sitting on the lumber are the Edith Dodd Culver (left) and Loa Lloyd Lees (right). Charlotte Jane Kennan Lloyd, Loa's mother, is sitting in the car to the left, with an American flag draped over the backseat. Edith was the new bride of Howard Paul Culver, a student pilot. She and Loa had gone to school together. Nearly every afternoon, Edith and Loa came over to the flying field to wait for their husbands' return. *Courtesy of the author.*

its regular fourteen hundred revolutions per minute. But that gasoline leak sobered everyone on the flight.

Close to landing, Macaulay throttled down as he got to eight hundred feet, the H-10's nose pointed down sharply. At his speed and rate of descent, it felt to the crew as if the water rushed to meet them. The H-10 glided as lightly as a feather into the waters of Hampton Roads as Macaulay chopped the power. Two and a half hours after the flight started, it was over.

Top speed of the Curtiss H-10, a fifteen-ton flying boat, was about 130 miles per hour on Macaulay's first attempt to reach Baltimore. The British government had earlier that year bought twenty H-10s from Curtiss. With a wingspan of seventy-six feet across and a body of forty-five feet long, it was an impressive aircraft. The airframe was the largest ever flight-tested at that time. Macaulay maintained an altitude of about one thousand feet, perfect for passengers trying to get a bird's-eye view of Hampton Roads and the Chesapeake Bay. The log of Macaulay's May 4, 1916 flight records his eleven world records and the new American mark for altitude for a plane carrying a pilot and five passengers. The log meticulously details the time, points and miles reached during the flight:

TIME	POINT	MILES
1:35 p.m.	"Up"	0
1:40 p.m.	Old Pt. abeam	4
1:43 p.m.	Thimble	$5\frac{1}{2}$
1:47 p.m.	Back River	6
1:53 p.m.	York Spit	$8\frac{1}{4}$
2:02 p.m.	Wolf Trap	$12\frac{3}{4}$
2:12 p.m.	Windmill Pt.	$14\frac{1}{2}$
2:26 p.m.	Smith Pt.	$19\frac{1}{2}$
2:33 p.m.	Pt. Lookout	$13\frac{1}{2}$
Here rain forced return.		
2:39 p.m.	Smith Point	$13\frac{1}{2}$
3:05 p.m.	Windmill Pt.	$19\frac{1}{2}$
3:22 p.m.	Wolf Trap	$14\frac{1}{2}$
3:34 p.m.	York Spit	$12\frac{3}{4}$
3:43 p.m.	Back River	$8\frac{1}{4}$
3:49 p.m.	Thimble	6
3:52 p.m.	Old Point	$5\frac{1}{2}$
3:58 p.m.	Newport News	4
	Total Miles	164

The twin engine H-10 had to be readied for Macaulay's May 1916 flight and is shown here anchored just off the seaplane ramp at the station being prepared for flight. *Courtesy of the Sargeant Memorial Room, Norfolk Public Library.*

Captain Baldwin had just sent a rowboat back to the H-10 to retrieve Theodore Macaulay, Stewart Cogswell and several mechanics when this picture was taken. *Courtesy of the Sargeant Memorial Room, Norfolk Public Library.*

Opposite: A Curtiss H-10 flying boat, its airframe not yet fully assembled and without its engines, was photographed inside an Atlantic Coast Aeronautical Station hangar, a rare view of a historic aircraft. But on May 4, 1916, Curtiss flight instructor and test pilot Theodore Charles Macaulay departed the Newport News station flying this H-10 flying boat and established eleven new world records and one new American altitude record for a plane carrying a pilot and five passengers. Macaulay's flight was the last great event to take place at Curtiss's renowned southern experimental center before America's entry into World War I. Macaulay set new marks for duration; distance, closed circuit; distance, straight line; speeds from ten to two hundred kilometers; and for greatest speed per hour flight of five kilometers. Until Macaulay's record-breaking 1916 flights with this aircraft, most of the world records he broke were held by France's Roland Garros. *Courtesy of the Sargeant Memorial Room, Norfolk Public Library.*

As they rowed back to the beach, the H-10 remained anchored in Hampton Roads. Jimmy Honor is the first man from the left in the rowboat, Theodore Macaulay is the second and Stewart Cogswell is seated at the far right. Less than two years after his record-setting flights, Captain Baldwin lost his star pilot to the war effort. Macaulay's World War I draft registration card listed his employer as the United States Army Signal Corps Aviation Service. He was one of the first civilian flight instructors at the corps' newly minted flight school in Chicago, Illinois. But in the spring of 1917, he was commissioned a first lieutenant and rapidly advanced in rank. Born in Minneapolis, Minnesota, on September 30, 1887, Macaulay stayed in the army air service after the war. He was still on active duty at the formation of the army air corps and the United States Air Force, from which he retired as a colonel. Macaulay died on April 19, 1965, in San Diego, California. *Courtesy of the Sargeant Memorial Room, Norfolk Public Library.*

The former world record for duration of one hour, twenty-four minutes, eleven seconds had been held by Garros of France.

Macaulay had the opportunity to make Baltimore on May 6, 1916. He scrambled a five-man crew that included Pomilio, Hall, Utter, Good and Curtiss photographer Frank Conway and left Newport News bound north for Fort McHenry, a distance of 178 miles. Macaulay reported to the wire services:

> *It looked as we took to the air with our crew of five at Newport News that we were destined for a rough trip. The sky was overcast and off Old Point. We ran into a shower. Soon passing beyond it, we were headed up the bay*

and on account of the haze our navigating officer, Lieutenant Norman Hall, of Norfolk, had his hands full keeping our bearings.

The behemoth flying boat made the Newport News to Fort McHenry run in three hours, three minutes, despite gale-force winds. Macaulay noted:

We reached the mouth of the Potomac at 9:24 and encountered at a 1,500 level our disturbed air condition. Climbing to 2,000 feet at the mouth of the Patuxent we discovered we were making almost no headway for over fifteen minutes. We dropped about 500 feet and flying at that altitude passed over several war vessels and the Yammacraw of the Coast Guard Service off Annapolis. Entering the Patapsco River at 10:43 and flying over Fort Carroll we landed in front of Fort McHenry at 10:51.

Members of Macaulay's crew seated in the forward cabin had their lunch off Annapolis and amused themselves computing the speed of the aircraft. By the time the H-10 and its crew touched down in Arundel Cove, the men were weary and in need of a good night's sleep. Though Macaulay planned to refuel and return to Newport News that day, the return trip was delayed when coast guard officers requested time to inspect the H-10 to see how it had endured the trip. As the largest flying boat in the world at that time, the Curtiss H-10 was under careful scrutiny. The coast guardsmen made Macaulay's crew "snugly comfortable" at the service's Arundel Cove station and proved themselves "wonderfully hospitable hosts." Yet despite the coast guard's abundance of caution, the May 7 return trip met with tragedy. As it passed over Washington, the H-10 plunged from one hundred feet into the Potomac River and killed Charley Good.

Charley Good's death didn't dampen international interest in Curtiss's H-10 or any of Curtiss's future Model H flying boats that would make their debuts in the years to come. The week after Macaulay's record-breaking flights from Hampton Roads, on May 8, 1916, he left for Russia. Moscow had consigned planes from the Curtiss Aeroplane and Motor Company, and Macaulay was sent over as an instructor pilot, continuing the work of Charles C. Witmer, Curtiss engineer and pilot, who had made several trips there in 1912 to deliver F-boats and provide instruction to Russian pilots. But Witmer was so captivated by the rapid advance of Russian aviation that in November 1914 he accepted an appointment to the Russian Airship Corps with headquarters in Sebastopol. Macaulay was also impressed that the Russians were beginning to overtake the French and Germans in aviation science. He just didn't want to live there.

The Curtiss H-1 *America*, built for Rodman Wanamaker's transatlantic attempt and thereafter the benchmark for all flying boats to follow, was christened on June 22, 1914, at Hammondsport, New York, by sixteen-year-old Katherine Masson. She is joined at the christening (from left to right) by Royal Naval Air Service Lieutenant John Cyril Porte, George Eustace Amyot Hallett and Glenn Curtiss. The *America* was painted red and was originally fitted with two ninety-horsepower OX-5 V-8 engines. *Courtesy of the George Grantham Bain Collection, Library of Congress Prints and Photographs Division.*

Macaulay was settled in Russia when American newspapers began to report the arrival at Newport News of parts of a behemoth flying boat for the British admiralty that Rodman Wanamaker would, once again, try to fly across the Atlantic. "The crossing of the Atlantic Ocean in one flight," Wanamaker wrote,

> *is, to my mind, as important to aerial navigation as was the voyage of Columbus to transportation by water. What man can do once, he can do any number of times. Once the Atlantic is crossed in a single flight of an airship, there will soon follow regular transatlantic trips and a fixed, safe transatlantic passenger airline. The crossing of the Atlantic by air is not a matter merely of initiative, not of daring, nor even of skill; it is a problem of science.*

His strong belief that he would be the man to make this happen is clear. The April to June 1916 *Independent* that carried Wanamaker's writings on the subject was published after parts of his Curtiss Wanamaker Model T triplane flying boat had already begun to arrive at Newport News from Buffalo.

The *America* first flew on June 23, 1914. Porte and Hallett are shown aboard the *America*. They were to pilot the *America* from the United States to England on August 15, 1914, but this plan had to be abandoned when war in Europe erupted on August 3. The *America* was sold to the British, and Lieutenant Porte used it as the basis for his Felixstowe F.5 flying boat. Not all was lost for Curtiss, either. He used the *America* as the leaping-off point to design bigger and better flying boats, from the H-12 and H-16 to the Model T. *Courtesy of the George Grantham Bain Collection, Library of Congress Prints and Photographs Division.*

Baldwin reported that it would take at least two months to assemble and test the triplane flying boat, the only one of its kind that ever existed. The January 13, 1916 *Scientific American* let its readers know that Curtiss's behemoth seaplane was, for lack of a better description, the world's first "battleship aeroplane" and a direct descendant of his *America*. "The Curtiss 'battleship aeroplane' is a triple-screw triplane flying boat," the magazine reported, "which will weigh, fully equipped, 21,450 pounds." The triplane's hull was constructed of cedar planking sheathed with copper on its underside and riveted to stout ash ribs. By the numbers, the Model T was sixty-eight feet long and had a beam of twenty feet. The hydroplaning surface of the hull was furnished with a V-shaped bottom, which ended in a straight stem forward, while its rear, cut off sharply, gave the triplane the "step" on which the boat must ride in order to get off the sea. From the step on the hull, it had straight side lines and tapered

Among the early picks for Wanamaker's behemoth triplane seaplane crew was Lawrence Burst "Gyro" Sperry, one of America's greatest aviation figures of the twentieth century whose inventions revolutionized the industry. Sperry, shown here in Washington, D.C., on March 21, 1922, in the prototype of his Sperry Messenger biplane, was the inventor of many flight instruments and other hardware still in use today, including autopilot, the turn and bank indicator, the parachute pack, retractable landing gear, refinement of the gyroscope his father invented and development of artificial horizon, still used on most modern aircraft. His greatest achievement for military aviation was the development of the aerial torpedo. But he died too soon. Born on December 22, 1892, in Chicago, Sperry was killed on December 13, 1923, when his Messenger went down over the English Channel, cause unknown. *Courtesy of the Library of Congress Prints and Photographs Division.*

gently toward the stern to end with a water rudder. Curtiss's engineers divided the hull into twelve watertight compartments, one-third of them designed to keep the aircraft floating should the hull be breached and several compartments flooded.

The fuel tanks could hold seven hundred gallons of gasoline and eighty gallons of oil, which gave it a cruise radius of 675 miles at a speed of 75 miles per hour. But this number could be considerably increased by fitting additional fuel tanks, in which case the crew would drop its military load, including guns and bombs. The wingspan was 133 feet. Curtiss originally designed the Model T with six 160-horsepower water-cooled, V-type engines that were coupled in twin units of 320 horsepower, each unit driving an

Philadelphia millionaire Rodman Wanamaker's greatest contribution to aviation was his financing of two classes of Curtiss experimental seaplanes, both intended for transatlantic flight. These were Curtiss's Model H and Model T. He is shown in this photograph of the period. *Courtesy of the George Grantham Bain Collection, Library of Congress Prints and Photographs Division.*

airscrew about 15 feet long. Wanamaker also invested in the latest navigation equipment, including wireless telegraphy. Curtiss and Wanamaker estimated a July or August 1916 transatlantic crossing would take thirty hours. An early pick to round out its crew of six was Lawrence Burst "Gyro" Sperry, one of America's greatest aviation figures of the twentieth century whose inventions had already revolutionized the industry.

The Wanamaker Model T's engine configuration continued to evolve well past Wanamaker's targeted date to make an Atlantic crossing. Curtiss redesigned it to carry four 250-horsepower Curtiss V-4 tractors in a straight line. But his Buffalo plant had to build them. In the meantime, Curtiss scrapped his plan to assemble and test the triplane in the United States. He shipped the airframe off to England without the engines. When it arrived, Curtiss agreed to mount it with four 240-horsepower French Renaults. The Model T, the first four-engine aircraft ever built in the United States, was successfully flown. Curtiss never built any more

The Curtiss H-12 flying boat shown here was built by the Curtiss Aeroplane and Motor Company and was affectionately called a "Large America" by its navy aircrew. This aircraft is significant as the next generation of large flying boats initiated after Rodman Wanamaker financed its antecedent *America* in 1914. The United States Navy ordered nineteen H-12 flying boats, which were far larger than anything in service when introduced to the navy in 1916. Originally equipped with two two-hundred-horsepower Curtiss V-X-X engines, some of the navy's H-12 flying boats were reengined with two four-hundred-horsepower Liberty 12s and redesignated H-12L. *Courtesy of the George Grantham Bain Collection, Library of Congress Prints and Photographs Division.*

Wanamaker Model T triplane flying boats. The same war that stole Wanamaker's dream to make a transatlantic crossing in 1914 denied him a second time in 1916. No successful transatlantic crossing was made until May 1919, when the United States Navy's NC-4 flying boat successfully completed the trip.

4

TO WAR WE GO

The year 1917 rode in on the wings of a dove named Ruth Bancroft Law, arguably the United States' foremost female pilot. She came to the Atlantic Coast Aeronautical Station on January 11 to watch Victor Carlstrom flight test a one-of-a-kind touring triplane, custom designed and built for her at Curtiss's Buffalo plant. She stood below and watched as Carlstrom soared several thousand feet over Hampton Roads, circling Newport News and Fort Monroe before bringing the aircraft back to earth. The triplane performed well, comfortably making over seventy-five miles per hour. With its narrow wings, wider fuselage and 110-horsepower engine, it was capable of doing better. Law wanted the triplane to attempt a transcontinental flight from San Francisco to New York. She was already world famous as the first woman to loop the loop in an airplane, as the first to make a night flight and as the one-time holder of the Chicago to New York aerial speed record. But the dove couldn't stave off the tide of war. What came next signaled the beginning of the end for Curtiss's Atlantic Coast Aeronautical Station.

America's involvement in World War I changed everything. The majority of Curtiss's best flight instructors and test pilots had joined the flying arm of the army and navy. Their decision was to be expected. Patriotic young men went off to war. The surprise came when their leader did the same. The "captain" in front of Thomas Scott Baldwin's name had always been honorary. But after he volunteered his services to the army, and they were accepted, he was commissioned a captain in the United States Army Signal Corps Aviation Section on April 25, 1917,

A Touring Triplane for Ruth Law

A new world's record is now in order

Wires are not entirely absent from the construction of the machine. But they are so few in number that their effect will be negligible. Resistance has been reduced by eliminating the rear struts

THE early builders of aeroplanes cared little for the resistance offered by the air. They were glad enough to fly at all. Wires and struts were used with no regard whatever for their retarding effect when propelled against the air at railway speed. The aviator sat on the lower edge of a biplane so that his body added its resistance to that of numerous projections. No wonder that monoplanes were swifter.

Soon aeroplane builders discovered what they should have known in the very first place—that it is easier to move a large, correctly designed bulk through the air than a multitude of projections each of which rakes the atmosphere and leaves a little wake of its own behind it. As a result the aviator, whether he mounts a monoplane or a biplane, is now completely enclosed in a kind of boat-body so shaped that it parts the air easily and leaves a comparatively quiet wake at the rear.

In the early days of the aeroplane, it was thought that the piling of surface on surface, while it meant stability in flying,

The boat body is so shaped that it parts the air easily and leaves a quiet wake behind

also meant much head-resistance. It is true that the resistance is increased. But if structural difficulties are overcome, wire stays may be abandoned without at all weakening the craft. Recently a triplane without wire staying broke the speed record of monoplanes—an achievement which would have been considered impossible only five years ago. The performance of that triplane served to drive home the lesson that it is head-resistance which counts for everything in attaining speed. After that success it naturally followed that a touring triplane like that of Miss Law should be built.

Study the photographs of Miss Law's machine. Wires are not entirely absent. They are necessary because of the machine's size. Still they are so few in number that their effect must be almost negligible. The rear struts have disappeared with the result that useless resistance has been much reduced. Plucky Miss Law, who accomplished so much with an antiquated type in flying from Chicago to New York, should do great things in this modern machine.

A one-off touring triplane was built especially for Ruth Bancroft Law by the Curtiss Aeroplane and Motor Company. The first time this aircraft ever flew was at Newport News, Virginia, on January 11, 1917. Law stood on the field at the Atlantic Coast Aeronautical Station that day and watched as test pilot Victor Carlstrom took it up. She clapped with delight as he soared several thousand feet over Hampton Roads and circled Newport News and Fort Monroe before bringing it back to the station. The triplane performed well, comfortably making over seventy-five miles per hour. With its narrow wings, wider fuselage and 110-horsepower engine, it was capable of doing better. Law wanted the triplane to attempt a transcontinental flight from San Francisco to New York. *Popular Science Monthly* (volume 90, January–June 1917) ran these images of Law and her triplane taken on the day of its test at Newport News.

Major William "Billy" Mitchell made regular trips to Newport News, Virginia, for flight instruction starting with his first flight on September 4, 1916. While most of his flight instruction was taken with Jimmy Johnson, Walter Lees also taught him. Lees (left) was photographed giving Mitchell (right) a flying lesson during a chilly weekend in the fall of 1916. The aircraft, often misidentified as a Farman F.40, is a Curtiss experimental aircraft, an attempt to improve on the Farman plane, which at that time was one of the most popular reconnaissance platforms in use by European and Russian aviation squadrons. *Courtesy of the Sargeant Memorial Room, Norfolk Public Library.*

This aircraft, photographed at the Atlantic Coast Aeronautical Station in the fall of 1916, has been misidentified as a Farman F.40 and a Vickers F.B.5. The station was used as a laboratory for Curtiss aircraft, and many of these unique aircraft were one of a kind. Side-by-side comparison would clearly show that a two-seat Curtiss JN-4 Jenny fuselage was cut off, sealed at the open end and reversed; its wings and landing gear were reconfigured; and its motor and motor covering were reengineered to convert this aircraft into a pusher. The plane, while similar in many respects to the Farman, is Curtiss's interpretation of one of World War I's most successful reconnaissance biplanes. *Courtesy of the Sargeant Memorial Room, Norfolk Public Library.*

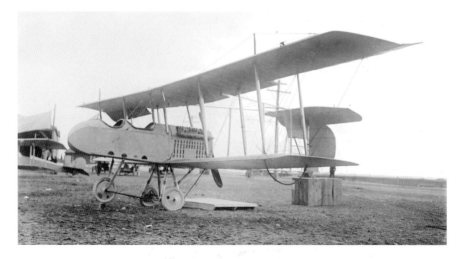

Glenn Curtiss was keenly aware of his competition for government contract. When he tinkered with the design of a competitor's aircraft, while speculative, it is likely because he saw room for improvement and the chance to sell a better product. This Farman-like Curtiss aircraft shares some elements with France's Farman F.40, introduced by Farman Aviation Works in 1915 and retired in 1922. During World War I, forty French Air Force escadrilles flew the F.40, also called a Horace Farman, and so did the British Royal Naval Air Service No. 5 Wing and the Russian Imperial Air Force. This aircraft also has features similar to the British Vickers F.B.5 gun-bus fighter, also introduced in 1915. *Courtesy of the Sargeant Memorial Room, Norfolk Public Library.*

This page and next: This fine-looking young man trained as part of the second group of the First Yale Unit. His face appears in a composite photograph of young men of the first and second groups of the First Yale Unit, many of whom ended up receiving their flight training and/or commissions in Hampton Roads. Many of these naval aviators returned after the war to finish their educations; others never finished at all, going only two or three years to college before heading off to war. Both photographs of this naval aviator were taken in November 1917 at Hampton Roads by Frank Conway and are certainly the correct time frame for those who were commissioned ensigns from the First Yale Unit. Even after consultation with the Manuscripts and Archives Department, Sterling Memorial Library, Yale University, no positive identification was made of this naval aviator by name. Though his picture here and in the unit photograph are a positive match, sadly no one has been able to put a name with the face. *Courtesy of the author.*

and honorary turned official. Baldwin remained in charge of the Atlantic Coast Aeronautical Station until August 31. Just two days before he left Newport News for good, Baldwin announced that he had recruited sixty civilian students for the flight training program, the first time the school was at full capacity since the United States Navy began phasing out its student naval aviators.

Baldwin received orders on September 13 to report to Washington, D.C., for duty in the office of the chief signal officer as head of Army Balloon Inspection

The Curtiss R-9 was a World War I advanced trainer. The aircraft shown here, Bureau No. A958, was photographed at Naval Air Station Hampton Roads on May 17, 1918. The navy bought 121 R-9s, and the army purchased an additional 10. *Official United States Navy Photograph.*

and Production. Nearly two weeks later, on September 24, Baldwin was sent to Akron, Ohio, to carry out his duties involving inspection of balloons and dirigibles. He personally inspected every lighter-than-air craft built for and used by the army during the war. Baldwin was promoted to major on June 18, 1918, and honorably discharged on October 25, 1919. He held three pilot certificates from the Aero Club of America: Balloon Pilot Certificate No. 1, Airship Pilot Certificate No. 9 and Airplane Pilot Certificate No. 7. He died in Buffalo, New York, on May 17, 1923.

Baldwin's departure was a sinking blow to Curtiss's Newport News operation. He'd lost the contribution of a trusted friend, and the flight school and test flight facility lost a leader. Stewart Cogswell was named as his replacement. He would have little left to manage after the army got Langley Field up and running and the navy established an air detachment, later air station, at Pine Beach on land formerly occupied by the 1907 Jamestown Exposition. The end of navy pilot training at Newport News

Ensign Cecil Dunmore "Mike" Murray, USNR, Naval Aviator No. 117, and Ensign Emory Arthur Stone, USNR, Naval Aviator No. 138, posed for Frank Conway in their flight gear. They are standing on the seaplane ramp, used by Naval Air Detachment Hampton Roads in November 1917. Both Murray and Stone trained at the Curtiss Flying School, Newport News, Virginia, prior to transferring to the detachment at Hampton Roads in June 1917. This provided a lengthy training period for budding naval aviators. *Courtesy of the author.*

Frank Conway took this picture of Ensign Cecil Dunmore "Mike" Murray, USNR, Naval Aviator No. 117, on the right, who posed with an unidentified crewman in November 1917. *Courtesy of the author.*

Ensign Cecil Dunmore "Mike" Murray, USNR, Naval Aviator No. 117, Naval Air Detachment Hampton Roads, was photographed by Frank Conway in November 1917. *Courtesy of the author.*

Ensign Charles Fairchild Fuller, USNR, Naval Aviator No. 139, was photographed by Frank Conway on the day he and his fellow student naval aviators were finally designated naval aviators in ceremonies held at Hampton Roads in November 1917. Fuller was officially designated on November 7, 1917, having completed his flight training at Curtiss Flying School in Newport News, followed by advanced training at Hampton Roads. Born on January 11, 1897, in New York City, New York, he attended the Harvard University class of 1919 and received a wartime degree in 1920. After Fuller left the navy, he obtained a bachelor's degree in architecture from Columbia University in 1924. He died in January 1960 at the age of sixty-three. *Courtesy of the author.*

Ensign William Bull "Bill" Atwater, USNR, Naval Aviator No. 112, took ground instruction and much of his flight training at the Curtiss Flying School at Newport News, Virginia, and was designated a naval aviator at Hampton Roads on October 19, 1917. Atwater was already an experienced flyer when he arrived in Hampton Roads. He learned to fly before entering the navy. Frank J. Conway took his portrait. *Courtesy of the author.*

officially came on August 28, 1917. But at a deeper level, beyond being squeezed out of business by the War Department, aviation research and development as Glenn Curtiss, Eddie Stinson, Orville Wright and all the other great aircraft makers had known it was over. An America at war could no longer rely on an industry that, prior to 1917, had yet to adopt

Ensign George Walter Shaw, USNR, was a 1917 graduate of the Curtiss Flying School, receiving pilot certificate No. 4. Since he was from Attleboro, Massachusetts, Shaw returned home to enroll as a quartermaster first class at Boston. He returned to Newport News later that year and was designated Naval Aviator No. 171 on November 13, 1917. Shaw was commissioned on November 26. This Frank Conway photograph was taken at that time. Shaw saw action in World War I and was awarded the Navy Cross as a seaplane pilot on patrol and convoy duty in the vicinity of Wexford, Ireland, and bombing a submarine under minimal flying conditions. Shaw went into partnership with Eddie A. Stinson Jr. in the Stinson Flyers, the first recorded commercial gypsy-flying circus in the United States. He barnstormed the country until 1930. *Courtesy of the author.*

Ensign Phillips Ward Page, USNR, Naval Aviator No. 170, struck a pose in the cockpit of a Curtiss N-9H floatplane for Frank Conway. Page was a Boston, Massachusetts native, born on November 28, 1885, making him much older than his contemporaries. This Harvard graduate attended Orville Wright's flying school after college graduation and earned his wings in 1912. From 1912 to 1917, Page went on the exhibition circuit as a pilot and instructor for the Burgess Company, of Marblehead, Massachusetts, and Curtiss Aeroplane and Motor Company, of Hammondsport and Buffalo, New York. *Courtesy of the author.*

automobile makers' assembly line process to push out aircraft. Prewar data show aircraft were built slowly and in small number.

The *Virginian-Pilot and Norfolk Landmark* ran a story on July 1, 1917, outlining Chairman of the Advisory Committee on Aeronautics of the Council of National Defense Howard Earle Coffin's plan to develop an entirely new type of airplane that, for the first time, would sacrifice speed in favor of aircraft armament. The Glenn Curtisses and Orville Wrights of aviation thought they had done mankind one better with the aircraft they had already produced. Orville Wright responded in a prepared statement that he and his late brother, Wilbur Wright, believed that when they made the airplane a success, they had also made wars impossible. Orville Wright observed:

> *If the Allies' armies are equipped with such a number of airplanes as to keep the enemy planes entirely back of the line, so that they are unable*

The United States Army rejected Phillips Ward Page's application for service since he was already thirty-one years old, too old for combat flying. The navy did not have the same reservations about his age and commissioned him an ensign on May 19, 1917. Page started as a flight instructor. He met all qualifications necessary to bear the title "naval aviator" by November 13, 1917, at Hampton Roads and was photographed by Frank Conway in front of the Curtiss N-9H floatplane. Fate wasn't kind to "P.W." Page. He reported to Paris, France, for initial assignment and was sent to Royal Naval Air Station Felixstowe, England, where he was killed on December 17, 1917, in an airplane crash. His body was never recovered. *Courtesy of the author.*

to direct gunfire or to observe the movement of the allied troops, it will be possible to end war.

In the summer of 1917, Orville Wright superintended the construction of a four-squadron aviation field at Dayton, Ohio, named for his brother, Wilbur. The original field on which the Wright brothers had built their first successful flying machine was located in the center of this new army airfield. "When my brother and I built and flew the first man-carrying machine [in 1903]," he iterated,

we thought that we were introducing into the world an invention which would make further wars practically impossible. That we were not alone in this thought is evidenced by the fact that the French Peace Society presented

Frank J. Conway took this photograph of three student naval aviators shortly before they were commissioned as ensigns in the United States Navy. They are (from left to right) Ensign Charles Fairchild Fuller, USNR, Naval Aviator No. 139; Ensign James Paul Warburg, USNR, who served in the naval flying corps but not as an aviator during World War I; and Ensign Westmore Willcox, USNR, Naval Aviator No. 136, of Norfolk. Within a five-day period between November 5 and 10, 1917, all three were commissioned, and in the two weeks that followed, Fuller and Willcox were designated naval aviators. Warburg, born in Hamburg, Germany, on August 18, 1896, was educated at Harvard University and after the war became one of the nation's most important international bankers. He served as financial advisor to President Franklin D. Roosevelt until becoming disillusioned with the New Deal and America's isolationism. The latter inspired him to reenter government service in 1941 as special assistant to coordinator of information Major General William Joseph "Wild Bill" Donovan, who became wartime chief of the Office of Strategic Services (OSS) and is widely recognized as the father of the Central Intelligence Agency (CIA). A year into World War II, Warburg was sent overseas as director of the Office of War Information propaganda policy. Warburg's tethers to the OSS and, later, CIA remained strong. He cofounded the Institute for Policy Studies in 1963. Warburg died on June 3, 1969. *Courtesy of the author.*

us with medals on account of our invention. We thought governments would realize the impossibility of winning by surprise attack and that no country would enter into war with another of equal size when it knew that it would have to win by simply wearing out its enemy.

Glenn Curtiss's southern investment, by 1922 sharing accommodations with the Newport News Aero Club, didn't fade quietly from the aviation

The United States Navy wasn't the only service with a growing aviation presence in Hampton Roads during World War I. The fledgling aviation section of the United States Army Signal Corps had Langley Field under development in December 1916, partnered with the National Advisory Council for Aeronautics (NACA), predecessor of NASA, and the navy to establish a joint airfield and proving ground for aircraft. Thus, Langley Field, now Langley Air Force Base, is the first military base in the United States built specifically for air power. The base's first buildings were surrounded by farmers' fields as far as the eye could see. A Curtiss JN-4D Jenny (left) and an experimental Curtiss S-3 triplane (right) had just been rolled out of wood and canvas hangars when this picture was taken in the summer of 1917. *Courtesy of the Library of Congress Prints and Photographs Division.*

scene. There had to be one more victim of the war. In the wee hours of the morning on May 11, 1922, the first aircraft theft in the United States took place when a World War I–period Curtiss JN-4D, privately owned by Hampton's Elmore Powell, was swiped from the aero club hangar. The popularity of private aviation grew exponentially after World War I. Many of the war's flyers turned to barnstorming and air racing when they returned home, and the public couldn't get enough. Powell had just spent $750 to buy himself an airplane. He figured the thief had to be someone he knew. After all, he thought, pilots weren't a dime a dozen, and it could only have been a couple of the nuttier ones who would be bold enough to pull that kind of stunt.

Roland Rohlfs began his career in 1914 as a mechanic with the Curtiss Aeroplane Company, first at Hammondsport and then at Buffalo. Later, he became a test pilot for the company after learning to fly at Curtiss's Newport News flying school. Victor Carlstrom was his flight instructor. *Courtesy of the Library of Congress Prints and Photographs Division.*

Opposite, top: This Curtiss S-3 experimental triplane, photographed in the summer of 1917 at Langley Field, belonged to United States Army Signal Corps Aviation Section and is marked "SC 323" to indicate this fact. The triplane was also photographed by Frank Conway at Curtiss's Atlantic Coast Aeronautical Station, where it was first assembled and tested before turnover to the signal corps. This is *not* the Curtiss 18-T Wasp triplane, also called a Kirkham, a two-seat fighter designed by Curtiss's chief motor engineer Charles B. Kirkham and manufactured by the Curtiss Engineering Corporation as two prototypes for the United States Navy designated A3325 and A3326. The triplane in this photograph was part of Curtiss's first attempt at a fast and maneuverable single-seat fighter. His first two variants of this aircraft, S-1 and S-2, were biplanes. But in 1917, the S-3, a modified S-2, became the first triplane in service in the United States. The wingspan on this aircraft is only nineteen feet, six inches, and it was powered by a one-hundred-horsepower Curtiss OXX-3 engine. Only one S-6 triplane, an improved S-3, was built for the signal corps the following year. *Courtesy of the Library of Congress Prints and Photographs Division.*

Opposite, bottom: As a point of reference, this *is* the Curtiss 18-T Wasp prototype. The aircraft was designed around the Curtiss-Kirkham K-12 water-cooled, twelve-cylinder engine of four hundred horsepower and sported an extremely clean aerodynamic design by contemporary standards, featuring a monocoque three-ply fuselage and side radiators positioned between the lower wings. Curtiss test pilot Roland Rohlfs, shown here with the Wasp, achieved a world speed record of 163 miles per hour carrying a full military load of 1,076 pounds when he flew the aircraft in August 1918. The Wasp set a new altitude record the following year when it reached 30,400 feet. Unofficially, the Wasp reached even higher altitudes when pushed. The Curtiss 18-T1 Wasp, a variant, is considered the top performing triplane of World War I, despite the fact that it never entered production as a service type. As the war ended, large aircraft contracts were cancelled, among them the navy's purchase of the Wasp. But by then, too, the triplane was out of vogue. The army and the navy wanted biplanes that could fly faster and farther. *Courtesy of the Library of Congress Prints and Photographs Division.*

Born in Norfolk, Virginia, Ensign Emory Arthur Stone, NRFC, Naval Aviator No. 138, was a British army officer before the United States entered World War I in April 1917. With America in the fight, he resigned his British commission and promptly joined the Naval Reserve Flying Corps. He was in training at Curtiss's Newport News flying school when he received his commission as a navy flyer and was designated an instructor at Hampton Roads. Assigned to Calshot, England, Stone was the pilot of a British seaplane engaged in convoy patrol on March 16, 1918, when they went down in the ocean in pursuit of a German submarine. As Stone and his observer clung to the aircraft, Stone released a carrier pigeon to summon help. They hung on for eighty-two hours without food and water before being picked up. He received the Navy Cross for bravery, courage and fortitude in pursuit of the enemy and for his survival at sea. *Courtesy of the author.*

William Gray "Billy" Schauffler Jr. was in flight training at Newport News from November 1916 to April 1917. Schauffler was born in Beirut, Syria, on November 24, 1891, to his physician father, a professor in the medical department of American University from 1891 to 1896. Still at Newport News, Schauffler and Curtiss instructor Carl Batts decided to deliver two "airmail" letters to the Newport News Golf Club. The stunt made all the newspapers. Schauffler was called to active duty on April 2, 1917, four days before the United States officially entered World War I. Captain Schauffler (standing) and Lieutenant Francis Adolph Tillman Jr. are shown here posed with their Ninetieth Aero Squadron fighter. As a first lieutenant, Schauffler was the squadron's first commander. He also designed the Ninetieth's Pair O' Dice emblem displaying natural sevens during this campaign, symbolic of the squadron's seven aerial victories against aircraft during the Saint Mihiel campaign. *Courtesy of the George Grantham Bain Collection, Library of Congress Prints and Photographs Division.*

Powell was wrong. He didn't know just then that his friend Russell Simon lost his Jenny, too. The *Times-Herald* ran a double-line header across the top of page one: "Airplane Thieves Steal Two Machines Here During Darkness" and "Wreck One Trying to Soar to Safety." The subheading filled in the blanks: "Think Reckless Drunks Behind Daring Affair." But even the newspaper was only half right. The thieves were two absent-without-leave airmen who had broken out of the Langley Field guardhouse and started the long walk to Curtiss's old flying field. James Brown and Atticus Hoppe

The sun was about to set on the Atlantic Coast Aeronautical Station and men like this one, who were part of the great chapter of aviation history written there. This unidentified aviator standing in front of a Curtiss JN-4D Jenny biplane trainer was photographed by Frank Conway at the end of 1916. *Courtesy of the author.*

Lawrence Leon, born in Torino, Italy, on June 15, 1889, immigrated to the United States in 1913. Three years later, he received Fédération Aéronautique Internationale Certificate No. 589 at Curtiss Field, Buffalo, New York. He served as flight instructor at the Curtiss Flying School, Newport News, Virginia, from January to August 1917 and as civilian instructor at various military schools until the end of World War I. In 1919, he traveled to Buenos Aires, Argentina, as the representative for Curtiss Aeroplane Export Corporation and spent thirteen years in South America as a business representative and flight instructor for Curtiss. Following his return from South America, he continued with Curtiss until 1940, when he left to pursue his own business opportunities. He died in Santa Clara, California, on April 26, 1965. Frank Conway took this photograph of him at Newport News. *Courtesy of the author.*

Among the famous who cultivated an association with Curtiss's Newport News flying school was composer, singer and lecturer Geoffrey O'Hara, best known for his wildly popular song, "K-K-K-Katy," which he wrote and then published in 1918. The song was billed as soldiers' and sailors' favorite goodbye song. Although born on February 2, 1882, in Chatham, Ontario, Canada, O'Hara had lived in the United States from 1904 and became an American citizen in 1919. This portrait was taken about 1910. *Courtesy of the George Grantham Bain Collection, Library of Congress Prints and Photographs Division.*

Geoffrey O'Hara's tenure at Newport News didn't make him a flyer. By the time America entered World War I, he was thirty-five years old and had long since given up on a military career. During the war, the United States Army sent him to Fort Oglethorpe, Georgia, to teach soldiers patriotic songs. He also did the same for the navy. Dressed in his army uniform without rank, O'Hara was photographed talking to a sailor. Though undated, the picture was taken during the summer of 1917. O'Hara died on January 31, 1967, at his Saint Petersburg, Florida residence. He was eighty-four. *Courtesy of the George Grantham Bain Collection, Library of Congress Prints and Photographs Division.*

may have been misguided in their actions, but they weren't drunk when they stole two aircraft. Neither of them was a pilot. When they couldn't get Powell's Jenny off the ground, they took Simon's. Brown got cold feet and wouldn't go along. But Hoppe took off. After a couple of turns over the field, he crashed on the beach upside down. Hoppe wriggled out of the wreckage unhurt, and he and Brown plotted their escape.

Powell's Jenny was found sitting in the middle of the runway, and further investigation revealed that Simon's was gone altogether. Simon did what anyone would do if his automobile were stolen from a driveway: he called the Newport News Police Department. The detective assigned

The most famous pilot in America before Charles Lindbergh's 1927 transatlantic flight from New York to Paris was Edward Vernon "Eddie" Rickenbacker, the United States' top fighter ace of World War I and a pioneer of commercial aviation. He was the recipient of the Medal of Honor and seven Distinguished Service Crosses. But he had also been a championship race car driver and automobile designer, owned the Indianapolis Motor Speedway and had been a government consultant on military matters. He'd done it all. Rickenbacker's colorful career crossed paths with Glenn Curtiss's Newport News facility. Rickenbacker is shown here with Frank Aloysius Tichenor Jr., son of the publisher of *Aero Digest* and *Sportsman Pilot*, at the White House on September 14, 1925. *Courtesy of the National Photo Company Collection, Library of Congress Prints and Photographs Division.*

Prior to issuance of the first wings of gold pin device on January 18, 1918, designated naval aviators had no clear form of identification other than their flying clothes. A change in uniform regulation dated June 22, 1917, called for the first uniform used exclusively by naval aviators: a summer-weight uniform similar to United States Marine Corps khaki. This uniform resembled service whites but could only be worn by officers involved in flying. The new uniform regulation also provided for the first flight suit, a coverall of canvas, moleskin or khaki the same color as the uniform, to be used only as flying dress. Naval aviators first assigned to Naval Air Detachment Hampton Roads donned many forms of this "flying dress." This Conway photograph shows another oddity of naval officer uniforms of this era: the naval militia or NNV insignia. This insignia was a circle around the star located on the shoulder board device. Taken in November 1917, this picture shows the naval militia insignia on the shoulder board of Lieutenant William O'Connell, USNR, head of the Hampton Roads detachment's aviation maintenance department. *Courtesy of the author.*

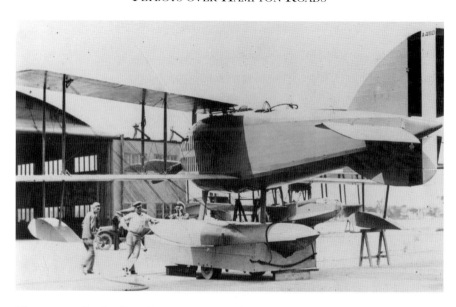

The two-seat Curtiss HA-1 Dunkirk fighter, shown here in 1919 at Naval Air Station Hampton Roads, was built for escort and air superiority. Only two were built for the navy, Bureau Nos. A4110 and A4111. The aircraft was originally test flown by Curtiss test pilot Roland Rholfs, who took it to thirty-five thousand feet. The Dunkirk had a four-hundred-horsepower Liberty engine and was equipped with dual synchronized machine guns forward and dual flexible machine guns in the rear cockpit. *Official United States Navy Photograph.*

Langley Field's new machine shop was state of the art at the time it was built. The footprint of this building was divided between assembly and repair. This picture was taken on May 20, 1923. *Courtesy of the author.*

Opposite, bottom: Without room to expand, the demise of the Atlantic Coast Aeronautical Station was sealed before World War I ended. The war years led to rapid development of Naval Air Station Hampton Roads and the army's nearby Langley Field. Present at Langley Field was the National Advisory Committee for Aeronautics (NACA), a federal agency established on March 3, 1915, to supervise and direct the scientific study of flight. By war's end, aircraft designers and the army and navy provided test pilots and aircraft to NACA for experimentation and flight test. Langley Field quickly overtook Curtiss's aeronautical station in size and importance. Langley sported this expansive airship hangar, photographed on September 3, 1920, from army airship ZD-1, formerly the Zodiac ZDUS-1, originally manufactured in France for the United States Navy and transferred to the army. *Courtesy of the Library of Congress Prints and Photographs Division.*

to find it didn't know where to start. But it didn't take long to locate the heap of fabric, wires and wheels on the beach at the end of the municipal small boat harbor. He checked with Langley and found out Brown and Hoppe had been detained at Camp Abraham Eustis, jailbirds once again. When they were later charged with grand larceny of an airplane, it was the first such charge ever made in the United States.

In nearly all respects, it is ironic that the story of Glenn Curtiss's Atlantic Coast Aeronautical Station ended with a theft. Theft is about what's taken away and often never returned. Metaphorically, World War I cut short what

New American Liberty twelve-cylinder engines were photographed inside Langley's machine shop on May 17, 1923. *Courtesy of the author.*

Flight training, experimentation and flight test previously performed at Newport News was now done at the navy's new air station on the Norfolk side and at the army air service field at Langley. Two Langley Field airmen prepared to make a double parachute jump from the top wing of this Army Air Service DeHavilland DH-4B AS63243, pictured here in 1922. The DH-4B was powered by the four-hundred-horsepower Liberty twelve-cylinder engine. *Courtesy of the author.*

During one of his rare 1916 visits to the Atlantic Coast Aeronautical Station, Glenn Curtiss was photographed by Frank Conway walking the length of the runway, a Curtiss JN-4D Jenny biplane soaring just overhead. Though this iconic photograph of Curtiss was taken at the beginning of his Newport News venture, it is also symbolic of the end of an era in America's storied aviation history. The station closed in 1922. *Courtesy of the author.*

"could have been." We were robbed of the possibilities. The era of glory that Curtiss brought to Newport News was over far too soon, carried away by men who turned those daring young men and their flying machines into swaggering fighter pilots over the skies of Europe.

SOURCES

E very effort was made to consult primary source material in the compilation of this volume, most especially official government and United States Navy and Army archives, including publications, records, original accounts, scrapbooks and photographic files found in the National Archives and Records Administration (NARA); Library of Congress (LOC); Smithsonian Air and Space Museum; Glenn H. Curtiss Museum; Department of Defense; Department of the Navy; Department of the Army; Naval Historical Center; National Museum of Naval Aviation; Hampton Roads Naval Museum; Portsmouth Naval Shipyard Museum; Casemate Museum; Virginiana Room, Newport News Public Library; Sargeant Memorial Room, Norfolk Public Library; and innumerable command histories, including unit and squadron histories and photographs. The rest was derived from the author's prior writings pertaining to and knowledge of the subject and her own collection of original documents and photographs. The author acknowledges the wealth of information gleaned from individual interviews.

INDEX

ABOUT THE AUTHOR

A nationally known, award-winning author of narrative nonfiction, Amy Waters Yarsinske received her master of planning degree from the University of Virginia School of Architecture and her bachelor of arts degrees in English and economics from Randolph-Macon Woman's College. She is a former president of the Norfolk Historical Society, cofounder of the Norfolk Historical Foundation and a graduate of CIVIC Leadership Institute. Yarsinske has over two decades of experience in the publishing industry as an author and editor and has made repeated appearances as a guest and commentator for major media, including American and foreign networks and international, national and regional radio markets. She is a member of Investigative Reporters and Editors (IRE), Authors Guild and American Society of Journalists and Authors (ASJA).

Yarsinske is the author of the widely read, award-winning *No One Left Behind: The Lt. Comdr. Michael Scott Speicher Story* (Dutton/NAL 2002, 2003; Listen and Live Audio 2002, 2004, 2006; Topics Entertainment 2004; Listen and Live MP3 2007; Playaway Digital Audio Player, 2009). She has published four prior works with The History Press: *Ghent: John Graham's Dream, Norfolk, Virginia's Treasure* (2006), *The Elizabeth River* (2007), *Lost Norfolk* (2009) and *The Navy Capital of the World: The United States Navy in Hampton Roads* (2010). Yarsinske is also the author of several aviation books, among them *Wings of Valor, Wings of Gold: An Illustrated History of U.S. Naval Aviation* (Flying Machines Press, 1998), *Mud Flats to Master Jet Base: Fifty Years at NAS Oceana* (Hallmark, 2001) and "Memories and Memorials," a chapter in *U.S. Naval Aviation* (Hugh Lauter Levin Associates, 2001).

also

{ AVAILABLE }

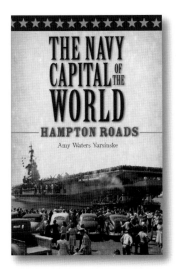

From the famous Civil War ironclads that clashed in its waters to the great battleships that gathered off Norfolk's Sewell's Point as part of President Theodore Roosevelt's Great White Fleet, the Hampton Roads region of Virginia has maintained a proud naval tradition. Into the twentieth century, the maritime region has remained on the cutting edge of military technology as the nucleus for the birth of naval aviation and the training site for scores of men who stormed the beaches of Europe and the Pacific during World War II. Through her fascinating research and incredible array of rare and striking photographs, military historian Amy Waters Yarsinske guides readers through the storied history of the navy in Hampton Roads.

RETAIL PRICE: $24.99   ISBN: 978.1.59629.973.3   LENGTH: 224 Pages

Visit us at
www.historypress.net